*Powers, Weakness, and the
Tabernacling of God*

Powers, Weakness, and the Tabernacling of God

THE 2000 SCHAFF LECTURES
PITTSBURGH THEOLOGICAL SEMINARY

Marva J. Dawn

WILLIAM B. EERDMANS PUBLISHING COMPANY
GRAND RAPIDS, MICHIGAN / CAMBRIDGE, U.K.

Wm. B. Eerdmans Publishing Co.
255 Jefferson Ave. S.E., Grand Rapids, Michigan 49503 /
P.O. Box 163, Cambridge CB3 9PU U.K.

Printed in the United States of America

06 05 04 03 02 01   7 6 5 4 3 2 1

Library of Congress Cataloging-in-Publication Data

Powers, Weakness, and the Tabernacling of God / Marva J. Dawn.
    p.   cm.   (The Schaff lectures / Pittsburgh Theological Seminary; 2000)
    Includes bibliographical references and index.
    ISBN 0-8028-4770-6 (pbk.: alk. paper)
        1. Church.   2. Powers (Christian theology)   I. Title.
    II. Schaff lectures at Pittsburgh Theological Seminary; 2000.

BV600.3.D39   2001
261 — dc21

                                                00-069195

www.eerdmans.com

This book is dedicated to

believers who make the hard choices, even in the face of doubts;
pastors who find themselves alone in resisting cultural tides;
Christian leaders who refrain from using methods of power;
saints who accept their weakness and let God use it;
churches who consistently nourish their neighbors;
prophets who never give up exposing idolatries;
disciples who display the presence of God;

and especially to Myron,
Trinity-bearer.

Contents

Acknowledgments

This book's themes coalesced when President Carnegie Samuel Calian invited me to give the Schaff Lectures at Pittsburgh Theological Seminary in March of 2000. I had been thinking about the biblical notion of the "principalities and powers" since my Ph.D. dissertation work starting in 1985 under John Howard Yoder at Notre Dame and about the "tabernacling of God in weakness" since my M.Div. thesis work under Wayne McCown at Western Evangelical Seminary in the late 1970s, but I had never before combined the two themes. I am especially grateful to President Calian for his gracious invitation and warm welcome and to Dr. Mary Lee Talbot, Director of Continuing Education at Pittsburgh Theological Seminary, and her assistant, Nancy Hammond, for their arrangements for my lectures and various kindnesses during my stay at the seminary. Particular thanks are due to all who contributed gifts of hospitality, wheelchair rides, and other types of assistance throughout my seminary visit. These acts of kindness were especially important because of the particular weakness that unduly afflicted me at the time of the lectures — an ulcerated injury to my left foot, which is normally encased in a leg brace, required that I be on crutches. This would have made the lectureship much more arduous without everyone's generosity. Those present for the lectures also gave fine feedback in the discussion periods; many of their comments and questions are reflected in these expanded pages.

I also want to thank Karyl Groeneveld, who in spite of back afflictions used her superior computer and lexical skills to give some exegetical suggestions that helped me as I updated my thesis work — and who now faces the ultimate weakness in her husband Doug's terminal cancer. May God shelter them in this time of grieving and pain and give them hope for the future tabernacling when sorrow will be no more.

Thanks are always due to Jennifer Hoffman, my superb and gracious editor, and to all the other stellar people at Eerdmans Publishing who help make my visions and crafted words into books.

Above all,
Soli Deo Gloria!

1 The Principalities and Powers: Created, Fallen, and Then?

Many events preceding our world's successful entry into the twenty-first century demonstrate the ubiquitous and ambiguous use made of the biblical notion of "the principalities and powers," both in societal and in religious discourse. Though a spiritual aspect is not usually on the surface when the language of "powers" is invoked, the immensity of these forces' influence suggests that the entities being discussed are more than merely human.

For example, just after Thanksgiving in 1999 somewhere between forty and sixty thousand peaceful marchers in Seattle, Washington, protested against the *economic powers* symbolized by the World Trade Organization. News commentators denounced the *political powers* of Osama bin Laden, whose threats of terrorism disrupted or disquieted many vacationers' plans, especially after one of his operatives was arrested in Seattle for possessing a very large bomb with the kind of exploding device used in the bombing of the World Trade Center in New York City. And in religious circles, fundamentalists of various sorts spoke of the millennial turn in apocalyptic terms and prepared for the last great battle against the *powers of evil,* usually perceived as personalized demons.

In all three cases, one contributor that greatly influenced people's attitudes toward these events was the *power of the media;* for example, the nature of the protests in Seattle was outrageously misrepresented. Television stations kept repeating video coverage of a small group of ruffians (not related to the major protests) who smashed windows and looted. Meanwhile, not one television newscast or newspaper report mentioned that there were more than sixty teach-ins offering hundreds of hours of workshops; that the Beneroya concert hall (used by the Seattle Symphony) was sold out for several teach-ins and speeches on peacekeeping and justice building; or that approximately forty different nonviolence training sessions were held by such groups as the Western Washington Fellowship of Reconciliation and New Society Trainers. My own brother and other nonviolent activists turned away as many as twenty people as they stood in front of stores to prevent vandalism and looting. These peaceful protesters knew that the *power of violence* is larger than the persons perpetrating it and sucks many into its tornadic funnel.

As Tom Yoder Neufeld observes in citing John Howard Yoder, Hendrik Berkhof, Walter Wink, and Miroslav Volf, these well-known commentators offer interpretation of the "powers" language that

> draws attention to how pervasive and insidious these powers are. As social, political, and economic realities the powers are diffused throughout the culture. Their demonic character rests not so much in their transcendent nature or personal agency, as in their capacity to control the imaginations and behavior of human beings, individually and communally.[1]

Why should we study the concept of "the powers" here, once more, now? The terminology seems to be pervasive again and reasonably well understood, thanks to the major efforts of Walter Wink. In my own past writings I have discussed the notion of "the powers" in order to raise ethical questions regarding issues that are not dealt with adequately if they are treated only on a material level, rather than with the spiritual response such evil requires.[2]

1. Thomas R. Yoder Neufeld, *Ephesians,* Believers Church Bible Commentary (Scottdale, PA: Herald Press, forthcoming), manuscript p. 463. Since Tom also respects the "ambiguity and implicit comprehensiveness" in the biblical use of "powers" terminology, I am very grateful to him for letting me see a copy of his commentary's penultimate manuscript. Future references will include manuscript page numbers, though undoubtedly numbers and perhaps citations will change.

2. See especially Marva J. Dawn, *Is It a Lost Cause? Having the Heart of God for the Church's Children* (Grand Rapids: Wm. B. Eerdmans Publishing Co., 1997), and Marva J. Dawn and Eugene H. Peterson, *The Unnecessary Pastor: Rediscovering the Call* (Grand Rapids: Wm. B. Eerdmans Publishing Co., 1999), particularly chapter 5. Since there is so much to explicate concerning the powers, this book will not duplicate previous discussions, except for brief summaries.

In this book I am particularly concerned to broaden the notion of "the powers" beyond Wink's emphasis on violence and to look especially at how this broader understanding will help us critique the misdirections churches are taking as they follow the methods of the culture around them. To do this, we will

- elaborate why "powers" language was lost in Christianity and how it was recovered;
- sketch an overview of the biblical description of the principalities and powers;
- outline various hermeneutical moves for appropriating the concept of "the powers" for present understandings;
- and consider briefly the churches' stance against other cultural powers.

Chapter 3 will offer examples of the principalities' fallen manifestations in churches in this new millennium. In Chapters 2 and 4 we will look positively at the Church's call to weakness as the *locus* of God's tabernacling and at what churches could be if they choose that weakness in order to resist the temptations of fallen powers.

The Recovery of the "Powers" Language

In a compelling chapter, "Christ and the Powers of Death,"[3] William Stringfellow commented in 1964 on the fact that the concept of "the principalities and powers" seemed to be lost in churches, but not outside of them (50-51). He told the story of one day when he spoke about the meaning of the principalities at the Business School of Harvard University after having discussed the matter earlier with students at the Divinity School. He noted that, though the students of the business school were not theologically trained, they "displayed an awareness, intelligence, and insight with respect to what principalities are and what are the issues between principalities and human beings." In contrast, the divinity students thought the biblical terms were "archaic imagery having no reference to

3. William Stringfellow, *Free in Obedience* (New York: Seabury Press, 1964), pp. 49-73. Page references to this book in the following paragraphs will be given parenthetically in the text.

contemporary realities" (51). The students' reactions confirmed String-fellow's recognition that the powers as a fallen, living reality (52) can be equated not only with institutions (55-57) but also with images (53-55) and ideologies (57-59).

The language of "the powers" fell out of use during the time of the Reformation, when various apocalyptic sects made Martin Luther and John Calvin cautious about eschatology. Then came a trend toward a non-cosmic and subjective conception of Christ's kingdom, a movement in which Friedrich Schleiermacher, Adolf von Harnack, Ernst Troeltsch, Johannes Weiss, and Albert Schweitzer were key figures. It is important to note this change: misunderstandings concerning the powers by certain groups induced the Reformers to exclude the language; in contrast, the later scholars rejected the concept itself because the work of Christ was reduced to inward dimensions. Both of these problems continue today and need to be addressed.

The notion of "the powers" began to be recalled, however, when there was no other way to name the extremity of events in the years surrounding World Wars I and II. One of the most widely influential leaders in restoring the vocabulary of "the powers" in theological discussion was Karl Barth,[4] although his work was preceded by that of Johann Christoph Blumhardt and his son, Christoph Friedrich Blumhardt.[5] The Blumhardts' witness that the lordship of Christ includes the social and political aspects of life had been largely unheard or misunderstood in their own time at the turn of the century, but began to be comprehended in the aftermath of World War I.[6]

Several years before the first scholarly treatments of the concept of "the principalities and powers," Dietrich Bonhoeffer wrote in 1932, "How can one close one's eyes at the fact that the demons themselves have taken over rule of the world, that it is the powers of darkness who have here made an

4. See Barth's *Rechtfertigung und Recht* of 1938, translated as *Church and State* by G. Ronald Howe (London: Student Christian Movement Press, 1939).

5. See *God's Revolution: The Witness of Eberhard Arnold,* ed. the Hutterian Society of Brothers and John Howard Yoder (New York: Paulist Press, 1984), pp. 14-15 (Arnold was greatly influenced by the Blumhardts), and *The Awakening: One Man's Battle with Darkness,* the story of Johann Christoph Blumhardt, told by Friedrich Zuendel (Farmington, PA: The Plough Publishing House, 1999).

6. See W. A. Visser 't Hooft, *The Kingship of Christ: An Interpretation of Recent European Theology* (New York: Harper and Brothers, 1948), pp. 15-31.

awful conspiracy."[7] Those who were trying to find language to describe the horrors of the times returned to the concept of "the principalities and powers" to express what went beyond modern psychological explanations.

Similarly, in the era of nuclear weapons and the cold war, the concept of "the principalities and powers" began to be used to describe the precarious situation of the world. For example, James W. Douglass insisted that "The 'powers' referred to by St. Paul are moving the world inexorably toward a global death. To deny that such is the obvious direction of the world is to succumb to idealism."[8]

Indeed, the horrors of modern Western civilization have required a closer look at the principalities and powers in order to formulate more realistically an effective Christian ethic for these times. Amos Wilder of Harvard asserted that the concept of "the powers," rather than obfuscating or impeding the relevance of New Testament eschatology or Christology, instead emphasizes the urgency of applying the gospel to the world of power structures in which we live.[9]

As the language of "powers" has been reintroduced to name the evils of our times, however, it has also been reduced in various ways — merely to "personal beings" or "demons," as popularized by the novelist Frank Peretti, or, on the opposite end of the spectrum, to institutions and structures, without regard for overarching supernatural dimensions. It is essential to recover here the larger frame of reference in the biblical record. The immense scope of the powers is suggested by William Stringfellow in *An Ethic for Christians and Other Aliens in a Strange Land,* in which he offers the following descriptions of the principalities:

- legion in species, number, variety, and name;
- creatures that are fallen (meaning that they thrive in chaos, confusion, and competition);
- an inverse dominion (one that works backwards — not to foster life, but to dehumanize);

7. Quoted in Bob Bowen, "Driving Out the Demons," *Gospel Herald* 78, no. 20 (14 May 1985): 337.

8. James W. Douglass, "On Transcending Technique," in *Introducing Jacques Ellul,* ed. James Y. Holloway (Grand Rapids: Wm. B. Eerdmans Publishing Co., 1970), p. 141.

9. Amos N. Wilder, *Kerygma, Eschatology, and Social Ethics,* Social Ethics Series No. 12, gen. ed. Franklin Sherman (Philadelphia: Fortress Press, 1966), pp. 23-34.

- not benign, but aggressive;
- causing all to be victims (with or without their knowledge);
- capturing leaders as acolytes enthralled by their own enslavement;
- engaged in rivalry with each other since their very survival is always at stake;
- and creating a new morality of survival.[10]

What ARE the Powers?

It is not possible in one short chapter to show adequately the wide divergence in interpretations of biblical passages concerning the principalities and powers.[11] Both because the language is used in a wide variety of ways in the New Testament texts and because of differing presuppositions on the part of scholars, there is extensive disagreement over such aspects as the nature or essence of the powers, how and when the powers might be defeated, and whether the powers will be ultimately destroyed or reconciled. We will consider only a few of the debates that are crucial for our purposes here.

10. William Stringfellow, *An Ethic for Christians and Other Aliens in a Strange Land* (Waco, TX: Word Books, 1973), pp. 77-94. In this book Stringfellow outlines probably the most thorough of all applications of the biblical texts about the powers to the experiences of contemporary life. He describes their character (pp. 77-94), their tactics (97-107), and their preeminent incarnation in the state, which needs to be demythologized (107-14).

Among the tactics that he specifies are these: denial of truth, doublespeak and overtalk, secrecy and boasts of expertise, surveillance and harassment, exaggeration and deception, cursing and conjuring, usurpation and absorption, diversion and demoralization, and the violence of babel (including verbal inflation, libel, rhetorical wantonness, sophistry, jargon, incoherence, falsehood, and blasphemy). Concluding by excoriating the state as the preeminent principality and the Antichrist in America, he also recognizes that these verbal tactics of "babel" aggressively intrude on Bible study in the churches — with the result that these workings of the powers prevent us from acknowledging the immense destructiveness of those very powers on the mission of the Church.

11. For a thorough explication of various debates over the biblical terminology, see Marva J. Dawn, "The Concept of 'The Principalities and Powers' in the Works of Jacques Ellul," Ph.D. dissertation, The University of Notre Dame, 1992 (Ann Arbor, MI: University Microfilms, #9220014).

The most important biblical texts concerning the powers offer us this sketch:

Colossians 1:16	The powers are created for good.
Romans 8:19-22	As part of the fallen creation, the powers share in its brokenness, participate in its destructions, overstep their proper bounds, and groan for release.
Romans 8:38-39	No matter how strong, the powers cannot separate us from God's love for us in Christ.
1 Corinthians 15:25-26	Death is one of the cosmic enemies to be subjected to Christ.
Colossians 2:13b-15	Christ disarmed the powers, exposed them, and triumphed over them.
1 Peter 3:22	Powers and authorities (grouped here with angels, which prevents us from losing sight of their larger dimensions beyond earthly materiality) are made subject to Christ.
1 Corinthians 2:8	The other side of the dialectic is given here: that earthly rulers (principalities) crucified the Lord of glory. This text also underscores the powers' functioning in religious, as well as political, spheres. This alerts us to the disturbing fact that *churches* today can similarly be principalities acting for evil instead of good.
Ephesians 6:10-20	We must stand against the powers and resist them by means of the armor of God. (This text is so critically important that we will consider it extensively in Chapter 4.)[12]

What kinds of truth does the imagery of the powers convey? This question has been clouded over by centuries of medieval and modern art and literature that interpreted the biblical concept graphically (and often erroneously). One thing seems sure, however. Oscar Cullmann stressed that the invariable mentioning of the powers in a decisive place in all of the ear-

---

12. An elaboration of the significance of these eight passages can be found in Dawn and Peterson, *The Unnecessary Pastor,* pp. 84-102 and 112-19.

liest formulations of faith (which provide the only objective criterion for determining what the first Christians considered essential) must cause us to recognize the importance for the early Church of Christ's victory over the powers.[13] I believe that it is crucial for churches in this new millennium to recover this doctrine — essential for the earliest Christians! — if we want to fulfill our true identity as Church.

Why Recognizing the Powers Is Essential Today

During the time when scholars were first recovering the notion of "the principalities and powers," James S. Stewart suggested in a path-breaking article still relevant today that something vital had been lost in Christian anthropology by the reduction of the concept to mere apocalyptic imagination.

Stewart claimed, first of all, that the sense of a cosmic battle manifested visibly on the stage of world events had been lost.[14] More significant, he continued, was the loss with respect to the doctrine of the atonement. Theologies stressing only the revelatory dimension of Christ's death have not taken seriously the New Testament focus on the demonic nature of the evil from which humankind must be redeemed. Thus, a basic component of the Christian gospel has been sidelined as extraneous. Stewart underlined this New Testament concentration as follows:

> The really tragic force of the dilemma of history and of the human predicament is not answered by any theology which speaks of the Cross as a revelation of love and mercy — and goes no further. But the primitive proclamation went much further. It spoke of an objective transaction which had changed the human situation and indeed the universe, the *kosmos* itself. It spoke of the decisive irrevocable defeat of the powers of darkness. It spoke of the Cross . . . as the place

---

13. Oscar Cullmann, *Christ and Time: The Primitive Christian Conception of Time and History,* trans. Floyd V. Filson (Philadelphia: Westminster Press, 1950), pp. 103 and 192.

14. James S. Stewart, "On a Neglected Emphasis in New Testament Theology," *Scottish Journal of Theology* 4, no. 3 (Sept. 1951): 293. Page references to this article in the following discussion are given parenthetically in the text.

where three factors had met and interlocked: the design of man,[15] the will of Jesus, the predestination of God. . . . [T]his three-fold drama can be understood only when the New Testament teaching on the invisible cosmic powers . . . is taken seriously and given due weight. (294-95)

This emphasis in Stewart is critical for my purposes here, for contemporary reductions of the doctrine of the atonement display the working of the powers themselves to diminish our understanding of the powers (as will be discussed in Chapter 3).

Stewart then analyzed the various elements of visible historic forces — namely, the *religious* leaders, Jewish and Roman *politics,* and the crowd (i.e., *social* forces) — which served as agents of more sinister invisible powers (295-96). Next, he showed why the concept of "the principalities and powers" is essential for understanding the incarnation, life, teaching, and ministry of Jesus as recorded in the Gospels. Only by meeting the cosmic forces on the ground of history where they were entrenched could Jesus break their power (297-99).

Finally, Stewart asserted that the only valid doctrine of the atonement could be one that is linked to a full New Testament Christology recognizing that God reconciled the world in Christ. Thus, the concept of "the principalities and powers" effectively eliminates dualism since the New Testament emphasizes, especially in Philippians and Colossians, that Christ has conquered the powers and displays his lordship over them (299-300).

Stewart's article underscores the importance for theological and biblical studies of restoring the concept of "the principalities and powers," but it does not contribute to helping us know how the question of the nature of the powers should be answered in the twenty-first century. We will look at several prominent approaches to that question next.

---

15. I apologize to readers who might be offended that a few of the authors quoted in this book — including Stewart and especially Jacques Ellul — did not use inclusive language. At first I modified and footnoted many changes, but realized that to do so sometimes changed the intent of the original writer. In the end it seemed that to impose our present standards of language on earlier literature is to be anachronistic.

The Range of Perspectives before Walter Wink

Cullmann's and Stewart's work underscored the critical importance of the concept of "the principalities and powers" for the Church's doctrine and life. But the difficult question remains of how the hermeneutical gap between this essential emphasis in the early Church and current theological directions can be bridged. Throughout the past fifty years interpretations of the notion of the "powers" have been spread between two poles. On one side were such scholars as Rudolf Bultmann, Ernst Käsemann, G. H. C. MacGregor, and Amos Wilder, all of whom agreed that the concept of "the principalities and powers" must be demythologized, though MacGregor and Wilder rejected the specific demythologizing of Bultmann. Most notably, in the first volume of his *Theology of the New Testament*, Bultmann calls the biblical statements about the powers "mythological" and asserts that the powers have no existence except for those who let them be significant.[16]

On the opposite end of the theological spectrum, and largely in reaction to the demythologizers, John Stott and others insisted that the Scriptures describe the powers as personal demonic beings and that this cosmology must be preserved.[17] Stott believed that to identify the principalities and powers with human structures causes us to "lack an adequate explanation [for] why structures so regularly, but not always, become tyrannical," to restrict unjustifiably our understanding of the malevolent activity of evil which is too versatile to be limited to the structural, and to "become too negative towards society and its structures."[18] Robert E. Webber modified Stott's position by claiming that the New Testament cosmology is viable, but that it recognized two kinds of powers — spiritual forces and the structures they use.[19]

Arguments for some sort of personal interpretation of the powers, however, too easily get caught up in the very speculation that biblical texts warn against. To counteract that tendency, D. E. H. Whiteley concluded

16. Rudolf Bultmann, *Theology of the New Testament*, vol. 1, trans. Kendrick Grobel (New York: Charles Scribner's Sons, 1951), pp. 257-58.

17. John R. W. Stott, *God's New Society: The Message of Ephesians* (Downers Grove, IL: InterVarsity Press, 1979), pp. 263-67.

18. Stott, *God's New Society*, p. 274. See John Howard Yoder's response to Stott in John H. Yoder, *The Politics of Jesus*, 2nd ed. (Grand Rapids: Wm. B. Eerdmans Publishing Co., 1994), pp. 160-61.

19. Robert E. Webber, *The Church in the World: Opposition, Tension, or Transformation* (Grand Rapids: Zondervan Academie Books, 1986).

from his extensive exegetical study that the Scriptures are more concerned with the "all-pervasive large-scale effects of the demonic-complex as a whole" than with "the activities of 'individual' evil spirits."[20] Other scholars, such as Heinrich Schlier[21] and F. F. Bruce,[22] brought together both poles by stressing that the powers might be encountered as individual personal beings or as collective entities.

Several theologians found other middle points between the demythologizers, who too easily identify the powers only with human structures, and the personalizers, who insist that the powers should be identified solely with angelic beings. Willem A. Visser 't Hooft, Cullmann, Albert H. van den Heuvel, Markus Barth, and Stringfellow[23] are among those who posit many correspondences between the biblical and contemporary worlds. Following Hendrik Berkhof, John Yoder suggests that certain concrete modern phenomena are "structurally analogous to the Powers"[24] but should not be equated with them. To show the broad range of such analogous phenomena, he lists religious, intellectual ("'ologies and 'isms"), moral ("codes and customs"), and political structures and claims that such an understanding enables the concept of "the principalities and powers" to provide a more refined analysis of the problems of society and history than is possible in theological descriptions that emphasize the "personality" of the powers.[25] In another work Yoder carefully nuances his description of the powers as follows:

20. D. E. H. Whiteley, *The Theology of St. Paul* (Oxford: Basil Blackwell, 1964), p. 27.

21. Heinrich Schlier, *Principalities and Powers in the New Testament* (New York: Herder and Herder, 1961), pp. 16 and 18-20.

22. F. F. Bruce, "Colossian Problems Part 4: Christ as Conqueror and Reconciler," *Bibliotheca Sacra* 141, no. 4 (Oct.-Dec. 1984): 299-300.

23. See Visser 't Hooft, *The Kingship of Christ;* Cullman's *Christ and Time;* Albert H. van den Heuvel, *These Rebellious Powers* (New York: Friendship Press, 1965); Markus Barth, *The Broken Wall: A Study of the Epistle to the Ephesians* (Valley Forge, PA: Judson Press, 1959), *Ephesians: Introduction, Translation, and Commentary on Chapters 1–3* and *Ephesians: Translation and Commentary on Chapters 4–6*, The Anchor Bible, vol. 34, parts 1 and 2, William Foxwell Albright and David Noel Freedman, gen. eds. (Garden City, NY: Doubleday and Company, 1974). Besides *Free in Obedience*, see also William Stringfellow's *An Ethic for Christians.*

24. Yoder, *The Politics of Jesus*, 2nd ed., p. 142.

25. Yoder, *The Politics of Jesus*, 2nd ed., pp. 142-44.

Now what these "cosmic authorities" were in Paul's mind is not easy to say in modern terms. They are not human persons. Yet they influence human events and structures. What we call the state, the economy, the media, ideology — these are their instruments.[26]

Though that description might support an exegetical move to name the principalities both as the human agents or structures (the "instruments") and as the authorities and powers that influence them, we must be very careful with Yoder not to set up a two-tiered cosmos if we delineate supernatural forces beyond the instruments they dominate.

Walter Wink's Notion of the Inside and Outside Aspects of Power

Certainly the name most often associated with investigation of the powers in our time is that of Walter Wink, whose five books on the powers are invaluable resources,[27] though I do think it is necessary to register some disagreement.[28] Wink credits William Stringfellow's *Free in Obedience*[29] for

---

26. John H. Yoder, *He Came Preaching Peace* (Scottdale, PA: Herald Press, 1985), p. 114.

27. Besides the three volumes of the trilogy discussed below, Wink has published summaries of his perspectives in *When the Powers Fall* (Minneapolis: Augsburg-Fortress, 1998) and *The Powers That Be* (New York: Doubleday, 1999).

28. Wink himself undertook his extensive investigation of the New Testament vocabulary out of critical disagreement with Wesley Carr's book *Angels and Principalities: The Background, Meaning, and Development of the Pauline Phrase hai archai kai hai exousiai* (Cambridge: Cambridge University Press, 1981). Wink is certainly correct that Carr's exegesis is faulty and his conclusions inappropriate. For example, because it does not fit his schema, Carr suggests that perhaps Ephesians 6:12 is an interpolation (p. 108), though there is not the slightest manuscript evidence for such a conjecture. Carr's earlier article, "The Rulers of This Age — I Corinthians II.6-8," *New Testament Studies* 23 (1976): 20-35, equally failed to take seriously the biblical text.

29. Among particular forms of the principalities Stringfellow describes in *Free in Obedience* are the fallenness of money, folk heroes, sex, fashion, sports, the crown, patriotism, and religion (59-60). After explicating the principalities as powers of death (64-70), he emphasizes Christ's victory over them (70-73). Later sections of the book describe the relationship of the church to the nations (83-89), the need for the church to stand against the principalities of the nations (89-95), and how the church often loses its freedom and becomes itself a principality (95-99). The book concludes with a

showing him the relevance of the powers for understanding institutional evil,[30] but he criticizes Stringfellow's work for its lack of precision since it seems to identify the principalities and powers only with structures.[31] Wink proposes the following preliminary observations:

1. The language of power pervades the whole New Testament (7).
2. The language of power in the New Testament is imprecise, liquid, interchangeable, and unsystematic (9).
3. Despite all this imprecision and interchangeability, clear patterns of usage emerge (10).
4. Because these terms are to a degree interchangeable, one or a pair or a series can be made to represent them all (10).
5. These powers are both heavenly and earthly, divine and human, spiritual and political, invisible and structural (11).
6. These powers are both good and evil (12).

After studying all the powers in the New Testament — *archē* (ruler) and *archai* (often translated "principalities"); *exousia* (authority/power); *dunamis* (power); *thronos* (throne); *kuriotēs* (ruling power); *onoma* (name); angels; fallen angels, evil spirits, and demons; and angels of the nations (13-35) — Wink adds this seventh hypothesis, which he claims is equally justified by the data:

7. Unless the context further specifies, we are to take the terms for power in their most comprehensive sense, understanding them to mean both heavenly *and* earthly, divine *and* human, good *and* evil powers (39).

Let me emphasize that Wink's survey of all the terms for the powers in the New Testament is extraordinarily helpful, as are many of his preliminary observations. However, it seems to me that some of his hypotheses

---

warning to the church to identify, expose, discern, and exorcise the powers of death by truly being the church (102-3) in envisioning and honoring the freedom of God (107-28).

30. Walter Wink, *Naming the Powers: The Language of Power in the New Testament*, vol. 1 of *The Powers* (Philadelphia: Fortress Press, 1984), p. xi. Page references to this book in the following discussion are given parenthetically in the text.

31. Stringfellow, *Free in Obedience*, p. 52. "What the Bible calls 'principalities and powers' are called in contemporary language 'ideologies,' 'institutions,' and 'images.'"

should be questioned. Though the terms *archē, dunamis, exousia, thronos,* and *kuriotēs* occur interchangeably on lists in the Scriptures, it seems that there are some differences between them and words for angels *(angeloi)* and demons *(daimonia)* — names that often seem specifically to signify supernatural beings. Wink's mixing together of all the terms confuses the meanings of these two sets, though the biblical usage suggests some precision in its choices from the two kinds of terms. Thus, Wink's proposition 4 — that all the terms are interchangeable and that one or more can represent them all — seems to be in error.

Similarly, Wink's examination of specific, key New Testament passages (40-96) fails to distinguish adequately between various terms. Though he concludes rightly that the ancients had a very rich and subtle awareness of the various forms of power (101), he does not himself explore that richness with an openness to characteristic nuances in word choices. He does not follow his own proposition 3 in attending to the "clear patterns of usage [that] emerge."

Wink rightly objects to the preoccupation in the past with the spiritual dimensions of the word field, which obscured the fact that the New Testament preponderantly uses power terms to refer to human and structural dimensions. Yet, he continues,

> it is precisely this spiritual aspect, in its very alienness to the modern worldview, that reveals how inadequate our categories are for interpretation. Scholars' instincts were not wrong, then, to focus on the spiritual dimensions of the Powers, but they tended to do so on an attenuated base. It is precisely this spiritual element which does not and cannot be made to fit our modern reductionist categories that most cries out for explanation. (101)

However, Wink's own investigation of the spiritual element falsely locates it only *within* the material structures and acknowledges no spiritual dimension *beyond* the natural. Similarly, though Wink also warns against the danger of making modern sociological theory and its unconscious ideological assumptions normative for New Testament reality, in the pages that follow these cautionary notes and especially in the second volume of his trilogy, Wink fails to follow his own advice.[32]

32. Wink's *Unmasking the Powers: The Invisible Forces that Determine Human Exis-*

His conclusion in the first volume is that the spiritual powers are not to be viewed as separate heavenly, ethereal entities but "as the inner aspect of material or tangible manifestations of power" (104). In arriving at this conclusion, Wink emphasizes the close intertwining of the inner and outer aspects by asserting that the spiritual realities have no existence independent of their material counterparts (105). Wink's point, then, is that, though the inner and outer aspects can be differentiated, they cannot be separated.

Rejecting as imprecise Cullmann's idea that the powers are *both* earthly *and* heavenly, Wink objects that his description suggests two different sets of agents, some human or institutional, others divine or demonic.[33] Wink emphasizes that what he is arguing instead is that

> the Powers are simultaneously the outer and inner aspects of one and the same indivisible concretion of power. . . . Instead of the old dualism of matter and spirit, we can now regard matter and spirit as united in one indivisible reality, distinguishable in two discrete but interrelated manifestations. (107)

Wink certainly is right to reject the false dualism of matter and spirit that is frequently imposed on biblical texts, but he is wrong thereby to eliminate entirely a different realm of spiritual forces separate from material agents. His conflation of the two reduces the cosmic battle in which we are engaged and thereby reduces the significance of the work of Christ and the Church's gospel proclamation.

Critique of Walter Wink's Perspectives

On the basis of my own exegesis and that of others,[34] I'm convinced that we cannot totally reject with Wink the notion of powers as supernatural entities nor agree with his theory which conflates them with their material

---

tence, vol. 2 of *The Powers* (Philadelphia: Fortress Press, 1986), seems to be much more Jungian than biblical.

33. Though Wink does not footnote it, he is probably referring here to Cullmann, *Christ and Time*, pp. 191-210.

34. See especially Yoder Neufeld, *Ephesians*.

counterparts. Various passages in the Scriptures seem to suggest that spiritual entities can exist even when not incarnated in matter.

My disagreements with Wink particularly concern the third volume of his trilogy, *Engaging the Powers: Discernment and Resistance in a World of Domination.* Frequently this book makes statements such as this: "But Satan, demons, and the Powers are rather later arrivals. Humanity was slow to perceive the spirituality of complex institutions and forces."[35] Such comments reduce the powers merely to our perceptions, rather than grasping that they are forces much larger than human energies, much more complex than human discernment, beyond merely the natural world. These forces might have been *named* later in Jewish history, but they certainly *existed* prior to their identification.

In general, Wink's handling of Scripture does not take texts seriously, as is demonstrated in his constriction of history in assertions that the creation, the fall, and the redemption are simultaneous (70) or that "'Fallen' simply means that we all live under the conditions of the Domination System" (72). "Fallen" means much more than that for sinful human beings and the whole creation, and the redemption fulfilled for us by Jesus requires a historical particularity that Wink wants to evade.

Wink has rendered inestimable service by calling our attention to the significance of the powers and the totality of their reign in present world structures, but his misreading of biblical texts misleads us. For example, he reduces Jesus simply to a person with immense integrity (e.g., 136-37) and diminishes the atonement to an idea confused by Paul (139-55). Wink himself is not thoroughly trinitarian and thereby elides an essential requirement for the atonement to be properly understood without ramifications of patriarchal oppression.

Wink is insightfully on target when he summarizes the Church's task in relation to the powers as this: "to unmask their idolatrous pretensions, to identify their dehumanizing values, to strip from them the mantle of respectability, and to disenthrall their victims" (though he fails to mention the Church's primary role in proclaiming Christ's victory over the powers). In these tasks the Church "is uniquely equipped to help people unmask and die to the Powers." But when Wink goes on to discuss "the char-

35. Walter Wink, *Engaging the Powers: Discernment and Resistance in a World of Domination,* vol. 3 of *The Powers* (Minneapolis: Fortress Press, 1992), p. 39. Page references to this book in the following paragraphs will be given parenthetically in the text.

ter of the church in its struggle with the Powers" as "published" in Ephesians 3:10, he again is too reductionistic in his insistence that "the heavenlies" are merely the "*interiority* of earthly institutions, systems, and structures" and that the churches' task is "to practice a ministry of disclosing the spirituality of these Powers" (164). We do disclose their spirituality, but the deadly combat against these "methods of the diabolical one" (my translation of Ephesians 6:11) is more than a battle against the inside of human constructions, and the battle is won because Christ has already conquered and invites us to participate in the reality of his reign.

Let me again underscore that Wink is extremely helpful to us in many respects. His chapter eight, "To Wash Off the Not Human: Becoming Expendable" (156-68), is essential, for, as he rightly understands, "Only those who have died to the Powers can make themselves expendable," which he asserts is "simply the meaning of baptism, with its renunciation of Satan and all his works" (163). However, since Wink has collapsed "Satan and all his works" to human entities, he hasn't really grasped the fullness of baptism in the gift of burial with Christ and resurrection to new life!

Ultimately, Wink seems to have reduced the powers to the problems of violence (which is, of course, partly what they are), but the way of Jesus is much more than nonviolence, and the battle against the powers includes exposing many more diabolical methods and much larger forces. Wink's collapse of the supernatural world of evil makes one wonder how much he has collapsed good and God.

Wink appropriately emphasizes the critical importance of prayer in responding to the powers. He recognizes that the first Christians did not blame God for their unmerited sufferings but instead sought by prayer and action to "bend evil back toward the purposes of God" (317). However, Wink's final chapter, "Celebrating the Victory of God," ends the book limply, because his hope is not based finally on the resurrection of Christ, and so his salvation is reduced merely to "the very struggle for liberation" in which "the powerless" discover "within themselves resources laid up by God in their creation" (323). That is not enough!

The feebleness of Wink's theology of the powers is made evident in his third-to-last paragraph:

That is why these inveterate and incurable singers cannot help joining their voices with the heavenly chorus, singing, "The kingdom of the world *has become* the kingdom of our Lord and of his Messiah,

17

and he shall reign for ever and ever" (Rev. 11:15). For *singing about* is a way of *bringing about.* (324)

He is right about the singing, but nowhere does Wink recognize that the Messiah, Jesus Christ, *has brought about* his kingdom in the (Triune) work of atonement and will ultimately bring it about in the recapitulation of the cosmos that Revelation describes, when all evil is ultimately destroyed in the fulfilling culmination of the kingdom of God. Wink's reduction of God makes his victory feeble; he loses the Joy of *Christ's* triumph over the powers at the cross and empty tomb![36]

Thomas Yoder Neufeld also recognizes that such treatment of the vocabulary of "the powers" is inadequate. He writes,

> Nevertheless, the line between human and divine or demonic realms is not a clear one, most especially in the case of the 'powers'. Col. 1.16 illustrates this by explicitly mixing the categories of visible and invisible, heavenly and earthly. The specific pairing of ἀρχαί καὶ ἐξουσίαι which heads up the list of powers in Eph. 6.12 appears ten times in the New Testament. In only three instances does the pair clearly refer to human authorities or institutions (Lk. 12.11; 20.20; Tit. 3.1). The other instances appear in the Pauline corpus: I Cor. 15.24; Eph. 1.21; 3.10; 6.12; Col. 1.16; 2:10, 15.[37]

Yoder Neufeld quotes Heinrich Schlier to show how he "evokes the ominous nature" of the powers well:

> The enemies are not this or that person, nor one's own self — they are not 'blood and flesh'. Naturally, blood and flesh can be found on the front lines of this battle (cf. 2.3). But the conflict runs much deeper. The struggle is finally against a myriad of tirelessly attacking opponents, too slippery to grasp, with no specific names, only collective designations. They are superior to humans from the outset through their superior position 'in the heavenlies', superior through

---

36. It is important to underscore that this is God's work and not ours!

37. Thomas R. Yoder Neufeld, *'Put on the Armour of God': The Divine Warrior from Isaiah to Ephesians,* Journal for the Study of the New Testament Supplement Series 140 (Sheffield, England: Sheffield Academic Press, 1997), p. 122.

their invisibility and their unassailability. After all, their position is an all-pervasive 'atmosphere' of existence which they themselves generate. They are all, in the end, inherently full of deadly evil.[38]

Yoder Neufeld continues,

This characterization of the powers prevents a choice between sociologically and politically identifiable 'powers' and those perceived as 'spiritual' and thus described mythologically. Both are intended. Better yet, the author of Ephesians would not have seen these as alternative categories, but as diverse manifestations of a seamless web of reality hostile to God. After all, as we are seeing, his understanding of the church participates as well in this mix of the human and the divine, the earthly and the heavenly.[39]

Finally, in a footnote Yoder Neufeld emphasizes,

The full scope and level of struggle is not comprehended if understood as a battle against human beings. . . . ch. 5 indicates that the battle against darkness and the forces of evil takes place within the conflicts and confrontations of social existence. It is in the realm of human interaction that the battle with the supra-human powers (also) takes place.[40]

Experiencing the Working of Evil in Multiple Forms

Very different from Wink's theoretical formulation is Johann Christoph Blumhardt's experience of evil's powers, as described in his biography, *The Awakening*, which has never gone out of print in its German version and is now newly published in English by the Bruderhof's Plough Publishing Company. This book details what happened when a quiet pastor, who had wondered already as a youth why the power of the gospel seemed so lim-

38. Heinrich Schlier, *Der Brief an die Epheser: Ein Kommentar*, 7th ed. (Düsseldorf: Patmos, 1971), p. 291; Yoder Neufeld is using his own translation.
39. Yoder Neufeld, *'Put on the Armour of God,'* pp. 123-24.
40. Yoder Neufeld, *'Put on the Armour of God,'* p. 124.

ited in his time, confronted the spiritual lethargy and various manifestations of evil in his congregation and village.

In his introductory overview of the biography, Günter Krüger describes how Blumhardt became involved in what he called "the Fight" against evil powers because

> he was ashamed at the thought of conceding power to the darkness affecting [his parishioner, Gottliebin Dittus]. Moreover, he pitied her. Little did he know that he had embarked on an uncharted spiritual journey that would last for the next two years. Taking the form of intense prayers and of terrifyingly real dialogues with demons that spoke through Gottliebin, this battle would demand all of Blumhardt's energies.[41]

The battle soon became extended as the same symptoms appeared in Gottliebin's sister Katharina. The Fight itself ended (and both women were restored to complete health, and spiritual renewal began soon thereafter) when "on the final night, a demonic voice howled, 'Jesus is the victor! Jesus is the victor!'"

> "Jesus is the victor!" That loud cry was heard throughout the village, and its echoes reverberated for the rest of Blumhardt's life — in his thinking, his preaching, and his pastoral work. And yet, whenever he would later be asked about the fight in Möttlingen, he played it down, insisting that it was not the battle itself, but what came afterwards, that was really significant.
>
> By Easter 1844 the entire town was swept up in an unprecedented movement of repentance and revival. The awakening spread beyond the town, too, into neighboring villages and farther afield in the Black Forest.[42]

The renewal led, on Good Friday in 1845, to an influx of visitors from 176 towns and villages at worship. The village blossomed with hospitality to receive all these guests, and many cases of healing were reported. Blumhardt recognized the working of evil not only in the demons exor-

---

41. Overview by Günter Krüger in Friedrich Zuendel, *The Awakening*, pp. 6-7.
42. Günter Krüger in Zuendel, *The Awakening*, pp. 6-7.

cised from the two women, but also in the spiritual lethargy that pervaded his congregation and the town before "the Fight" began.

The actual experience of exorcism of demonic entities separate from human embodiment, which is certainly attested profusely in other nations of the world, confirms our objections when Wink wants to reduce the biblical language to his "inside/outside" formulation. In Karl Barth we find a better tool for dealing with the hermeneutical issues than Wink and his predecessors provide.

Karl Barth and the Biblical Concept as Demythologizer

The demythologizers of the concept of "the principalities and powers," led by Bultmann, reject the notion that these "authorities" are personal supernatural beings, while those who insist that they are such beings often fail to recognize that Paul himself was trying to demythologize the notions of hierarchies of intermediaries in the culture of his time. Karl Barth recognizes this and turns the whole issue of modern hermeneutical problems on its head.

In some of his last lecture fragments, Barth uses the images of *The Sorcerer's Apprentice* to describe the powers as "spirits with a life and activity of their own, lordless indwelling forces . . . [which] escape . . . [and] are entities with their own right and dignity . . . as absolutes."[43] He admits that their reality and efficacy are obscure, ambivalent, and unintelligible, and he comments on their transitoriness and the variety of forms they assume in the different periods of history, in the various circles of culture, and in the lives of individuals. Above all, he insists that their reality and efficaciousness cannot be ignored (215).

Barth refuses to accept the criticism that the worldview of the New Testament authors was "magical." Instead, he claims that they were less hindered by the cosmology of their contemporaries than we are and thus "have in fact . . . seen more, seen more clearly, and come much closer to the reality in their thought and speech, than those of us who are happy possessors of a rational and scientific view of things" (216-17). They were

43. Karl Barth, *Church Dogmatics* IV, *The Christian Life*, trans. Geoffrey W. Bromiley (Grand Rapids: Wm. B. Eerdmans Publishing Co., 1981), p. 214. Page references to this book in the following discussion are given parenthetically in the text.

freely able, consequently, to take into account the reality and efficacy of the powers. Barth concludes that what is necessary is a demythologizing, not of the concept of "the principalities and powers," but of the myths of the modern powers, such as the state or mammon. By means of their myths the powers are able to exert their tyranny, which Barth describes at length (220-33).

Though Barth provides no exegetical basis for his conclusions, his argument that the Scriptures should demythologize the modern world certainly coincides with what we can find in studying Colossians 2 and passages in Ephesians especially. Christian truth is the first weapon listed for the battle against the powers, and the victory of Christ on the cross consisted in exposing the powers and making them vulnerable. The biblical concept of "the principalities and powers," therefore, though not clearly understood in our time nor precisely explicated by the biblical writers, can be brought into the twenty-first century as a means for demythologizing the actual powers of our times. That leads to several questions that are asked in the debates about the modern application of the concept and that are useful for our purposes here.

Issues of Application

Much of the contemporary discussion about the concept of "the principalities and powers" focuses on the need to apply it to postmodern realities. For example, William Stringfellow complains that Christians, whose biblical roots should make them wiser,

> remain . . . astonishingly obtuse about these powers. . . . Yet to be ignorant or gullible or ingenuous . . . , to underestimate the inherent capacities of the principalities, to fail to notice the autonomy of these powers as creatures abets their usurpation of human life and their domination of human beings.[44]

My concern in these chapters is for Christians to estimate rightly the capacities of the powers so that they do not lead us and our churches astray. It is also essential that we recognize that each church — as one of

44. Stringfellow, *An Ethic for Christians*, p. 17.

the created powers — constantly wrestles with its own fallenness and often fails to live by the power of the Holy Spirit in genuine fulfillment of its true vocation.

As one step in bridging the hermeneutical gap that sometimes causes us not to take seriously the importance of the concept of "the powers" for our ecclesiology, let us notice the many similarities between the biblical times and our own. Fifty years ago, for example, Gordon Rupp noted these parallels, which are still apparent today: a world that becomes too complicated too fast; a world in which the "little people" feel themselves to be playthings of great historical forces; a failure of nerve; the revival of superstition and religion, on the one hand, and, on the other hand, a growing sense of fatalism and reckless gambling upon wild chance. To these must be added all the strains and stresses of present advances in warfare, the great systems of power, the huge number of people, the immense quantities of material, the catastrophic facts that statesmen, economists, and politicians cannot even understand, much less control, so that "'things' still go bump in the night in an ever more frightening crescendo."[45] Finally, Rupp lists the inexorable bondage of the will of peoples and individuals; the idealisms of revolutionary movements, twisted and perverted solidarities, and ideologies; and the adventism, pessimism, despair, nihilism, and *Ausweglosigkeit* (or hopelessness because all approaches to solving a problem have been tried and failed; thus, the lack of a way out), which are the price of wishful and superficial thinking. All these are part of our *Schicksalzusammenhang,* or the interwoven bundle of forces that determine the common fate in which we are bound, including, for our purposes here, its pattern of evil.[46]

If all these parallels continue to exist between the biblical times and our own, one might ask if the victory of Christ over the powers claimed in the Scriptures has made any difference in the world. Thus, the first issue we must address as we consider the application of the concept of "the principalities and powers" must concern the status of the powers in light of the cross. Then we will assess the issue of their transformation. Finally, we must ask how individual Christians and churches should deal with the powers. All of these are important considerations prior to our investiga-

45. Gordon Rupp, *Principalities and Powers: Studies in the Christian Conflict in History* (New York: Abingdon-Cokesbury Press, 1952), p. 16.

46. Rupp, *Principalities and Powers*, pp. 13-26.

tion of how churches manifest characteristics of fallen powers and how the Church must "stand against" the powers outside and within itself for the sake of its true vocation.[47]

The Status of the Powers in Light of Christ's Victory

Some very old debates concerning our present relation to the powers have actually become more urgent these days as all kinds of questions are raised about the meaning of Christ's atoning work on our behalf. To look closely at what scholars have said in the past will help us see the importance of the issues for present doctrine and life in the Church.

One of the contested conclusions of Clinton Morrison's 1960 foundational study of Romans 13 and the powers was his assertion that the redemptive work of Christ concerns only the believers' attitudes and not a definite victory over the powers. He asserted that if the actual *exousiai* (the "powers") are taken to be the objects of Christ's work, then "the distinction between the realm of his authority (all things from the beginning) and the locus of his victory (those who believe) is lost," which leads to these consequences:

> (a) Creation in Christ and the work of Christ are applied to the same object; apparently either the second was unnecessary or the first inconsequential. (b) The cosmic application of Christ's work only demonstrates its failure, for nothing happened to the State or sin and death as such. (c) The work of Christ and the eschatological consummation are identically described (by blending Col. 2.15, Phil. 2.9d., I Cor. 15.28); evidently the first work was ineffective, and the 'once for all' event must be *repeated* as the eschatological triumph . . . , or was the latter event to be only a formality?[48]

---

47. Throughout this book I will use capitalized *Church* to signify the ideal as Christ would have his Body be and uncapitalized *church* or *churches* to name concrete fallen (and seeking to be faithful) realities.

48. Clinton D. Morrison, *The Powers That Be: Earthly Rulers and Demonic Powers in Romans 13.1-7*, Studies in Biblical Theology No. 29 (Naperville, IL: Alec R. Allenson, 1960), p. 139.

You might want to reread that paragraph several times to see its profound implications. If Christ really conquered actual powers themselves (a possibility that Walter Wink thinks is eliminated because he reduces the powers to merely the inside/outside of material institutions), then Morrison forces us to ask (a) What is the difference in the effect on the powers between the original creation and Christ's suffering and death? (b) Was Christ's death for nothing, since nothing in "real" life and time seems to be changed for the better? (c) What is the difference between Christ's work in history and the final fulfillment of God's purposes at the end of time? Was the first ineffective? Or is the last meaningless?

Morrison's first objection is commonly repeated today by theologians and pastors who do not seriously acknowledge the tragic consequences of the fall. Because the powers (as well as we) are rebellious, the work of Christ is not reduced to being unnecessary even though it is applied to the same object as the creation, nor is the creation rendered inconsequential. Rather, the fall of human beings into sin changed the status of creation, and it had to be restored.

In response to Morrison's second objection, we can indeed affirm a cosmic application of Christ's work, even though nothing *appears* to have changed; Christ's death is significant not only for individuals but for the sake of the reconciliation of the entire cosmos, including all the powers. John Yoder stresses that the lordship of Christ is a structural fact, not limited to those who have accepted it. He shows us the momentous implications of this point as follows:

> It was Johann Christoph Blumhardt who rediscovered for German Protestantism a century ago the wondrous power of the gospel in individual lives and at the same time the eschatological foundation of Christian involvement in politics. We may echo his battle cry: "Dass Jesus siegt ist ewig ausgemacht. Sein ist die ganze Welt!" "That Jesus is conqueror is eternally settled: the universe is his!" This is not a statement concerning the benevolent disposition of certain individuals to listen or of certain Powers to be submissive. It is a declaration about the nature of the cosmos and the significance of history, within which both our conscientious participation and our conscientious objection find their authority and their promise.[49]

49. Yoder, *The Politics of Jesus*, 2nd ed., p. 157.

It makes an enormous difference in the way individuals and churches live if we recognize that the entire atoning work of Christ (including his life, suffering, death, resurrection, and ascension)[50] has already made the cosmos his. Then our political involvement operates not from the need to change things, but from the desire to make clear what *really* is the case. (We will consider implications of this especially in Chapter 4.)

Both Morrison's second and third points are counteracted by a careful understanding of eschatology. Visser 't Hooft emphasizes the striking fact that the New Testament authors do not find a contradiction between the victory achieved once for all and the victory still to be won, and he uses Théo Preyss's phrase "objective dialectic" to describe this togetherness of the two aeons. A merely futurist eschatology undervalues Christ's victory and makes him only a potential king. On the other hand, an interpretation that sees only a victory already achieved underestimates the reality of the principalities and powers as adversaries and loses the hope of the end of salvation history.[51] The objective reality of both poles of the dialectic must be preserved and held in tension for the whole truth to be seen.

This objective dialectic is clearly seen in the distinct difference in emphases between the letter to the Colossians, which proclaims Christ's superiority over the powers in creation (1:16) and his victory over them in redemption (2:14-15), and the epistle to the Ephesians, which warns about the continuing warfare against the powers (6:10-20). Oscar Cullmann has made clear that this is only an apparent contradiction, that the situation of everything in redemptive history is very complex. But the complexity has its roots in a temporal, and not a metaphysical, dualism.[52] That is, Colossians is not talking about the situation in "heaven," as opposed to Ephesians' description of the struggle "on earth." Rather, Colossians displays the fullness of the new aeon, which has already broken into ours, while Ephesians does not let us forget that we still live with and in the old aeon, too.

As we keep this "objective dialectic" of Christ's victory in mind, let us

---

50. For an outstanding and thorough explication of the importance of the ascension for our understandings of Christ and the Church, see Douglas Farrow, *Ascension and Ecclesia: On the Significance of the Doctrine of the Ascension for Ecclesiology and Christian Cosmology* (Grand Rapids: Wm. B. Eerdmans Publishing Co., 2000).

51. Visser 't Hooft, *The Kingship of Christ*, pp. 80, 82-83.

52. Cullmann, *Christ and Time*, p. 199.

also carefully distinguish various points in time and the results in reality at each point. Three distinct time references in the biblical narratives must be held in view: (1) the point in time (at the cross and empty tomb) when the powers were defeated and became subject to Christ's lordship; (2) the continuing struggle in time during which the powers seek to become emancipated from that lordship; and (3) the future consummation of Christ's victory. The defeat of the powers is understood as a past fact, a present experience, and a future hope. This threefold character, G. B. Caird emphasizes, can be seen in the array of all the New Testament passages about Christ's victory over the powers. The time references are marked by the resurrection, the parousia, and the time in between.[53]

Though the victory over the powers on the cross was decisive, the battle against them must continue through time, since the powers rage in their struggle to be emancipated. Hendrik Berkhof compares this reality to the situation of the "hunger winter" in the Netherlands in 1944-45, when the Nazis, already defeated, were still oppressing the Dutch.[54] There was a change in the objective reality of the Nazis (as there was for the powers in Christ's work, contrary to Morrison), for their sovereignty had been broken and a limit had been set to their working — which was the sign and the promise of their ultimate and total defeat. In the same way the sovereignty of the principalities and powers has been broken, and it is the task of the Church to proclaim that. The working of the powers is limited, and it is the task of the Church to display that. Finally, this broken sovereignty and limitation are the signs of the ultimate defeat of the powers, and the Church is the place where those signs are celebrated, as we will see in Chapters 3 and 4.

How Did Jesus Relate to the Powers?

How shall the Church reveal the shackling and subjugating of the powers? Since we are followers of Jesus, of course we must look to his behavior as a model. In the 1953 lectures that formed the basis for *Church Dogmatics*

---

53. G. B. Caird, *Principalities and Powers: A Study in Pauline Theology* (Oxford: Clarendon Press, 1956), p. 80.

54. Hendrik Berkhof, *Christ and the Powers*, trans. John H. Yoder (Scottdale, PA: Herald Press, 1962), p. 43.

IV/2, Karl Barth specified these aspects of Jesus' model: he did not align himself with any of the political powers, nor did he set up an opposing party. He did not "represent or defend or champion any programme. . . . He was equally suspected and disliked by the representatives of all such programmes." He "set all programmes and principles in question. And He did this simply because He enjoyed and displayed . . . a remarkable freedom." He lived with all the orders and did not present any sort of "system" opposed to them. "He simply revealed the limit and frontier of all these things — the freedom of the kingdom of God."[55]

Correlatively, John Yoder stresses that the community of those who seek to follow Jesus will be the primary social structure through which other structures can be changed and that the pattern is one of "creative transformation" through "revolutionary subordination."[56] Thus, the powers will be neither destroyed, nor "Christianized," but rather "tamed."[57]

The process of "taming," however, is readily recognized by scholars and in our daily life and the work of our churches as an ongoing struggle. Markus Barth asserts that some changes do indeed take place, and at the same time he gives a realistic appraisal of the continuing struggle in the following description:

> The saints will learn that institutions, if made "to know" their place, can change. A state can cease from open or secret persecution of the Church. It can change from a tyrannical and chaotic order to a more dignified one that respects the freedom and right of both society and the individual. . . . As one form of institution follows another, it seldom can be held that each time the newer is better in all respects than the older, or that it will remain any better in the future. But at least, what was old and wicked and foolish had obviously and publicly to yield, to give in, and to change. And the newer institutions and orders will change, technology too, when signs of rebellion prove them to be against Christ's throne.[58]

55. Karl Barth, *Church Dogmatics* IV/2, *The Doctrine of Reconciliation*, trans. Geoffrey W. Bromiley (Edinburgh: T. & T. Clark, 1958), pp. 171-72.

56. Yoder, *The Politics of Jesus*, 2nd ed., pp. 185 and 162-92.

57. Yoder, *He Came Preaching Peace*, p. 114.

58. Markus Barth, *The Broken Wall*, pp. 230-31.

This is possible, he concludes, neither because Christians can make the powers good (by Christianizing them) nor because they can bring them into subjection to Christ, but because Christ is already their Lord.

What Must Our Churches Be in Relation to Other Powers?

Before we look at what the Church must be in its own identity as a power, let us consider how Christians as a Body relate to the powers. Though, as we have seen, there is much disagreement among scholars about the being of the powers, there is much greater agreement, but with differing emphases, concerning how to deal with the powers. This is due to the fact, as Heinrich Schlier emphasizes, that the whole attitude of the New Testament differs from that of Judaism and the surrounding Hellenistic world. Not only is the New Testament much more reserved, but also there seems to be no theoretical or speculative interest in the powers. There is no exact description, no hierarchical differentiation as in Judaica. Rather, the realm of the powers is of interest to the New Testament authors only because they must be resisted, because the authors are sure that in the victory of Christ their own ability to withstand the powers is assured, and because the Church is now the realm through which the powers continue to be defeated and by which their final end is foreshadowed.[59]

Indeed, we cannot dismiss the notion of "the powers" or call it "archaic cosmology." We must not fail to recognize its crucial importance for our understanding of how to "be Church." As John Yoder emphasizes in the epilogue added to his chapter on the powers in his revision of *The Politics of Jesus,* "The growing bulk of serious social thought using these concepts [of 'the powers'] . . . should be sufficient demonstration that the Pauline vision is realistic and illuminating." He especially stresses the point

> that this Pauline vision is far more nuanced and helpful than much contemporary discussion about "the problem of power" in Christian social ethics. . . . The Pauline perspective is far more clear about the intrinsic complexities of institutional and psycho-dynamic structures, such that basically good creaturely structures can nonetheless be oppressive, and basically selfish decisions can sometimes nonethe-

59. Schlier, *Principalities and Powers in the New Testament,* pp. 13-14, 40, and 52.

29

less have less evil outcomes. . . . The challenge to which the proclamation of Christ's rule over the rebellious world speaks a word of grace
is not a problem within the self but a split within the cosmos.[60]

Furthermore, though it is the responsibility of each Christian to understand the importance of spiritual warfare against the powers, it is crucial
for our times that Christ's victory over evil must be realized not only by
Christians in isolation, but especially by communities of believers. That is
why the New Testament is so concerned that churches remain an alternative society, not fostering the parasitic growth of the powers of evil but
maintaining purity and freedom. G. B. Caird calls for a "solidarity of
grace."[61]

In an explication of the powers that was designed for young adults in
the turmoil of the 1960s, Albert H. van den Heuvel, then the executive sec-
retary of the World Council of Churches Youth Department, offered a
thorough description of the response of the Christian community to the
powers. His sketch serves as an excellent introduction to the remainder of
this book.

First of all, he emphasizes that, since the powers have become structures of domination, they enslave people in new servitudes.[62] One focus of
the churches' task, therefore, must be to restore the freedom that God intends.

Churches recognize that the powers are like runaway horses that must
be controlled. They are unmasked, stripped of their semi-divinity, and
humbled through Christ's victory (69) on the level of Christians' daily lives
and work. No pat answers can be given beforehand for all the practical
questions this might involve. Sometimes solutions to situations can be
found; at other times the Christian community must continue asking
questions and trying to avoid wrong answers (108). Rather than unthink-
ingly committing themselves to their society or simply vegetating in it,
Christians are called to participate critically (109).

Van den Heuvel forces his readers to ask themselves honestly if they
want to participate critically, if they are able to bear the tension or the

---

60. Yoder, *The Politics of Jesus*, 2nd ed., p. 161.
61. Caird, *Principalities and Powers*, p. 84.
62. van den Heuvel, *These Rebellious Powers*, p. 61. Page references to this book in
the following discussion are given parenthetically in the text.

loneliness that this will create in their lives (110). This is a question I want also to ask of you. Are you willing to do what it takes to stand against the powers invading our churches? Are you *really*? I will ask these questions again at the end of this book, for one key to the vitality of the Church will be the transfer of ideas about the powers into actions and prayers against them!

Critical participation necessitates knowledge of and sympathy for the culture that dare not deteriorate into either a blind acceptance of reality or a refusal to take it seriously (111). The Christian community's rejection of the powers must be demonstrated (113), and its stories of Christ's over-powering of the powers must be told (118). Van den Heuvel compares this task to that of the child in "The Emperor's New Clothes," whose cry, "But he has nothing on at all!" gives courage to others and wakes them up as well (118). All of this must take place, furthermore, in the context of com-passion and forgiveness. Van den Heuvel confesses that in postwar Europe Christians "did not clothe ourselves in the proper garments of compas-sion, gentleness, humility, and patience. We often turned our victory into a rebellious power, and so the story started all over again" (134).

Finally, van den Heuvel emphasizes that Christian worship involves many dimensions of the community's work in relation to the powers. Ideally, the sermon should name them and demonstrate their perversions. The offering attacks the power of money. The intercessory prayers remind us of our task to be agents of God's reconciliation and commit us to live out our confession of faith in Christ's victory over the powers. The sacra-ments of baptism and the eucharist give signs and seals that we partici-pate in the triumph of Christ so that the powers have no ultimate control over us (134-35). Karl Barth calls this the "priestly function of the Church."[63]

Dale Brown explicates this practically when he reminds us again that the Christian community must be willing to pay the price of its witness to the powers. Key texts outlining the role of the Christian community in re-lation to the powers are Ephesians 3:7-10, which declares that the Church makes manifest to the principalities the manifold wisdom of God and the fact that their dominion has come to an end, and Mark 10:42-45, which re-minds the Christian community that it is only in being truly a servant Church, a countercultural model, that the people of God can demonstrate

---

63. Barth, *Church and State*, p. 66.

the need for and value of alternatives to reform and replace fallen structures.[64]

Most important, the Christian community must keep proclaiming the gospel of hope — not turning away from the darkness, but finding in the midst of it the light of Christ. The Church's unique message is that the only source of hope is God and not the powers. To manifest this wisdom requires not a Zealot-like effort to bring the powers to their knees, nor a Herod-like stance of collaboration, but a nonconforming servanthood that includes these tasks:

- submitting to, honoring, and praying for the powers;
- prophetically preaching the gospel of repentance to the structures;
- participating in the transformation of the structures;
- opposing structures when necessary;
- offering counter-structures where feasible;
- disarming the structures in preaching Christ crucified;
- and holding fast to the promises of God in spite of the powers.[65]

Finally, it must be explicitly stated that the struggle of the Christian community's life in dealing with the powers is made possible by the gift of the Holy Spirit. The Church's dependence upon the Holy Spirit must be explicitly affirmed here since the majority of scholars discussing the concept of "the principalities and powers" do not mention its importance.

William Stringfellow is one scholar who does emphasize the necessity of the Holy Spirit and of spiritual gifts for dealing with the powers. In his chapter "The Efficacy of the Word of God as Hope," he stresses that the gift of discernment is basic for living biblically and that the charismatic gifts provide the only powers Christians can use against the principalities and powers. Above all, he proclaims the importance of vigilance and consolation as essential attributes for biblical living and insists that ethics, then, will be sacramental, rather than moralistic, pietistic, or religious.[66]

These summaries prepare us to look more closely at the true character and vocation of the Church (Chapter 2), the mistakes of churches who adopt

---

64. Dale W. Brown, *Biblical Pacifism: A Peace Church Perspective* (Elgin, IL: Brethren Press, 1986), pp. 121-22 and 128-30.

65. Brown, *Biblical Pacifism,* pp. 130-31.

66. Stringfellow, *An Ethic for Christians,* pp. 138-46 and 152.

the world's powers and thereby function themselves as fallen powers (Chapter 3), and the life of churches who follow faithfully their true vocation as a created power witnessing to Christ's victory over the powers (Chapter 4). As James Luther Adams discerns, the actual working in history of the principalities and powers was specifically identified by the biblical accounts in the totalitarian state, the traditions of the gentiles, the legalism of the Pharisees, popular public opinion, and the customs of idolatry — all of which brought bondage and decay, hatred and injustice. In exposing these principalities and powers, the biblical writers pointed, as did Jesus, to a fundamental purpose of the authentic Church. The true Church will be a community alert to the struggle against these destructive forces and aware of the availability of the power of the Lord that overcomes or at least cripples them.[67]

Adams's listing of specific powers in biblical times reminds me of Mahatma Gandhi's litany of seven Social Sins:

> politics without principle
> wealth without work
> commerce without morality
> pleasure without conscience
> education without character
> science without humanity
> and worship without sacrifice.

These seem to be descriptions of present principalities and powers having overstretched their bounds. If, however, we are thinking about politics, personal economics, corporate economics/business, the entertainment industry, the educational system, the scientific industry/medical complex, and other contemporary powers, we must ask if churches that worship without sacrifice have anything to say to them.

One of my main points in this chapter has been that Wink is wrong to reduce the powers in such a way that we do not recognize that they are indeed creatures, with a life and integrity of their own.[68] This is crucially im-

---

67. James Luther Adams, "We Wrestle Against Principalities and Powers," in *The Prophethood of All Believers*, ed. George K. Beach (Boston: Beacon Press, 1986), pp. 168-69.

68. Many other commentators posit such an independence. See William Stringfellow's *An Ethic for Christians*, pp. 78-80, and his *Free in Obedience*, pp. 52-53.

portant because, as Bill Wylie Kellermann contends, that gives us the right to ask of each power whether it is fulfilling its particular vocation to praise God and serve human life.[69] In the following chapters we will ask what is the particular vocation of the Church (Chapter 2) and how that vocation is not (Chapter 3), and how it could be (Chapter 4), fulfilled.

69. Bill Wylie Kellermann, "Not Vice Versa. Reading the Powers Biblically: Stringfellow, Hermeneutics, and the Principalities," *Anglican Theological Review* 81, no. 4 (1999): 677-78.

2 The Tabernacling of God
and a Theology of Weakness

This chapter might seem to be totally disconnected from the previous one and the following two, but it actually is the critical core of this book. We cannot discuss (as we will in Chapter 3) the ways in which churches demonstrate their fallenness as powers, nor how to be true to our real power (Chapter 4), unless we understand the Church's calling to be the agent of God's purposes and the community of people among whom the Triune One dwells. If the Church is to be the place where God is found and from which God's purposes are furthered, then how does a congregation embody the Trinity's presence? What is the Church's true vocation as a created power?

The biblical understanding of power stands in sharp contrast to that of the early Greeks, who saw power as a cosmic principle and, as such, synonymous with the idea of god. The world was perceived as a manifestation of myriads of forces working in, by, and on it. Human beings had to find means to participate in these forces in order to survive — as can be seen in the many Greek and Roman myths about the relationships of human beings with various gods.

The world of the First Testament[1] was radically different primarily because of the Hebrew witness to the character of God. Knowing *YHWH* pri-

---

1. I join many scholars and pastors in calling the first three-fourths of the Bible the "First Testament" or the "Hebrew Scriptures," to avoid our culture's negative connotations of the name *Old* Testament and to emphasize both the consistency of God's grace for all God's people and also the continuity of God's covenants in the Bible first with Israel and then in addition with Christians.

marily as a God of history, rather than only of nature, gave rise to Israel's trust in a personal and caring God. Power was exercised by this God on behalf of the people, especially in the foundational event of the Exodus.

Similarly, in the New Testament, the climactic event of the resurrection, coupled with the entire narrative of the passion, demonstrates God's power on behalf of the people who are thereby liberated. Consequently uses of the idea of power on the part of Christ's followers tend to emphasize that the saints serve by means of Christ's power at work through them by the gift of the Holy Spirit.

God's Power *(dunamis)*

The word *dunamis* is used forty-one times in the New Testament to ascribe power to God. Although many of these instances are general acknowledgments of God's might and do not need to be considered here, it is important for us to see how Luke and Paul use the term, in contrast to the other Gospel and Epistle writers.

John never uses *dunamis* at all, and Matthew and Mark use it only in phrases ascribing power to God and in connection with the right hand of power. Luke, on the other hand, observes the power of God especially in the conception of Jesus by means of the Most High's overshadowing, and consequently he affirms that the child would be called the Son of God in a unique way (Luke 1:35). Furthermore, Luke notes that Jesus returned from the temptations in the wilderness by the power of the Spirit (4:14) and that it was by the power of the Lord upon Jesus that he was able to heal (5:17). Finally, in both Luke and Acts (24:49 and 1:8, respectively) he records the promise of the special pouring out of the power from above which the disciples were to receive after Jesus' ascension. Thus, for Luke, God's power is available to human beings and works through them.

Human (and Christ's) Weakness *(astheneia)*

The apostle Paul frequently conjoins his discussions of God's power with a recognition of human weakness, *astheneia* (including that of Jesus). The word *astheneia* occurs twenty-four times in the New Testament; nine times it refers to physical illness, and fifteen times it is used in a larger sense. All the Gospel uses of *astheneia* refer to infirmities and diseases, as do the uses in Acts, but the apostle Paul's use of *astheneia* is distinctive.

In the first letter to the Corinthians Paul immediately speaks of his *astheneia* as he reminds the believers there of the weakness, fear, and much trembling with which he had first come to them (1 Cor. 2:3; also Gal. 4:13). Later, in the great resurrection chapter, he rejoices that the body which "is sown in weakness will be raised in power," even as its dishonor will be changed to glory (1 Cor. 15:43). In Romans 8:26 he assures his readers that the Holy Spirit helps us in our weakness, evidenced by our not knowing how to pray, for "that very Spirit intercedes with sighs too deep for words."

The term *astheneia* is used by Paul six times in 2 Corinthians 11:30–13:11a. Three times he boasts in his weakness (11:30; 12:5; and 12:9), and once he writes of his contentment in times of weakness, mistreatment, and persecution (12:10). The reason that such rejoicing is possible is declared in 13:4 where Paul proclaims this great fact of the gospel: that in his weakness Christ was crucified, but that by means of God's power he continues to live. This is God's way: that through his *astheneia* Christ gave himself up to death — totally emptying himself and becoming obedient to the worst of deaths, as the letter to the Philippians asserts (2:5-10). Such a totality of weakness, of perfect submission to the will of the Father (as frequently recorded in the Gospel of John) makes possible the perfection of God's tabernacling in the world through Christ.

Weakness and *Teleō*

My interest in a theology of weakness began in the early 1970s when I was leading Bible studies for students at Washington State University. Reading the only commentary I possessed, I discovered that in 1937 R. C. H. Lenski had suggested that the verb *teleō* in 2 Corinthians 12:9 had been mistranslated. Instead of the Lord saying, "My grace is sufficient for you, for my strength is made perfect in weakness," he proposed that it should be rendered, "for the power is brought to its finish in weakness."[2]

Closer etymological studies seem to suggest that Lenski is right about the verb, though a survey of the literature uncovers no other commentator

2. R. C. H. Lenski, *The Interpretation of St. Paul's First and Second Epistles to the Corinthians* (Minneapolis: Augsburg Publishing House, 1937), pp. 1302 and 1305.

who supports such a conviction. However, my own exegetical studies convinced me that Lenski is wrong in the way he pursues his insight — because he continues to think of "power" in terms of the Lord's. (The Greek text of 2 Cor. 12:9 contains no pronoun in connection with *hē dunamis,* "the power."[3]) Interpreting the power as Paul's rather than God's leads to significantly different theological conclusions that are very important here for our discussion of being Church in a world characterized by the workings of various principalities and powers.

Utilizing several related word studies, my M.Div. thesis explored the distinction between the two verbs *teleō* and *teleioō* — the former meaning primarily "to end, finish," and the latter involving a wide range of connotations, including "to perfect, to make genuine, to complete, to succeed fully, to initiate, to make happen, to become."[4] The latter is used nine times in

---

3. Ralph P. Martin in the Word Biblical Commentary for 2 Corinthians (Waco, TX: Word Books, 1986) translates *teleō* as "fulfilled" but adds the pronoun *my* to signify the Lord's power (pp. 418-22). Ernest Best in the Interpretation series, *Second Corinthians: A Bible Commentary for Teaching and Preaching* (Louisville: John Knox Press, 1987), simply translates the phrase "my power is made perfect in weakness" (p. 120). Frederick W. Danker in *II Corinthians,* the Augsburg Commentary on the New Testament (Minneapolis: Augsburg Publishing House, 1989) states, "The words *made perfect* render the verb form τελεῖται, which expresses completion: 'is carried out'" (p. 195).

Victor Paul Furnish acknowledges in his Anchor Bible commentary that the *teleō* used in 2 Corinthians 12:9 is usually rendered "is brought to completion" or "to its goal," but he asserts that here the usage is different. He remarks that the power could be God's or Christ's, but he never envisions that it could mean Paul's, so he translates the verb "is made fully present" — a rendering that seems to me to be the opposite of Paul's intention in choosing *teleō* rather than *teleioō* (*II Corinthians: Translated, with Introduction, Notes, and Commentary,* The Anchor Bible [Garden City, NY: Doubleday, 1984], pp. 530-31). Though Paul Barnett realizes that verse 9 in 2 Corinthians 12 is the climax to the entire epistle, he follows the usual translation of the verb and adds "Christ's" in brackets (*The Second Epistle to the Corinthians* [Grand Rapids: Wm. B. Eerdmans Publishing Co., 1997], p. 572).

It seems to me that — in the absence of a pronoun before the word *power* — the idea that it is Christ's or God's is so engrained in people's minds that no one ever questions whose power it is, so other possibilities have to be found for translating a verb meaning "to end."

4. See Johannes P. Louw and Eugene A. Nida, eds., *Greek-English Lexicon of the New Testament Based on Semantic Domains,* vols. 1 and 2 (New York: United Bible Societies, 1988). This lexicon's approach and methodology make use of the insights of modern linguistics, and its definitions are based upon the distinctive features of meaning of a

the letter to the Hebrews, which portrays Christ as the perfect fulfillment of the priesthood and the tabernacle. *Teleō*, on the other hand, is used frequently in the book of Revelation, which includes many instances of terminating something, or carrying something out to the full. Paul uses the verb *teleioō* only once, and he uses it to emphasize that he has not reached the state of perfection implied by the verb. Rather, he insists, he continues to run his course and to discipline himself in order to press on toward the mark of the upward calling of Jesus Christ (Phil. 3:12-13).

The verb *teleō* seems to be more limited in its connotations. Out of twenty-eight instances in the New Testament, twenty-five times it is translated with verbs signifying some sort of finishing or ending or accomplishing. Of the remaining three, two appearances of the verb are related to taxes (Matt. 17:24 and Rom. 13:6) and reflect a common idiom, "to complete the taxes," which corresponds to our expression "pay taxes." The only other instance is the one in 2 Corinthians 12:9, which has always been rendered "to make perfect." It is my contention that this instance should not be excepted. Rather, the verb *teleō* here should be given the usual rendering, "to finish." Such a rephrasing would allow us to develop more clearly an understanding of the concept of God's power at work in human weakness.

Here is a listing of all the usages of *teleō* in the New Testament:

Matthew 7:28	Now when Jesus had finished saying these things
Matthew 10:23	"you will not have gone through [finished going to] all the towns . . ."
Matthew 11:1	Now when Jesus had finished instructing his twelve disciples
Matthew 13:53	When Jesus had finished these parables
Matthew 19:1	When Jesus had finished saying these things
Matthew 26:1	When Jesus had finished saying all these things
Luke 2:39	When they had finished everything required by the law

particular term in comparison with, and in contrast to, other related words in the same semantic domain. Definitions from this lexicon will be marked throughout this book with the number of the semantic field and the particular number of the word cited — e.g., the nuances given above for *teleioō* are *SD* 88.38, 73.7, 68.22, 68.31, 53.50, and 13.18, respectively.

Luke 12:50	"what stress I am under until it [the baptism] is completed!"
Luke 18:31	"everything . . . written about the Son of Man . . . will be accomplished"
Luke 22:37	"this scripture must be fulfilled in me"
John 19:28	when Jesus knew that all was now finished
John 19:30	When Jesus had received the wine, he said, "It is finished."
Acts 13:29	"When they had carried out [completed] everything that was written about him, they took him down from the tree and laid him in a tomb."
Romans 2:27	Then those who . . . keep [fulfill] the law will condemn you
Galatians 5:16	Live by the Spirit, I say, and do not gratify [fulfill] the desires of the flesh
2 Timothy 4:7	I have fought the good fight, I have finished the race
James 2:8	You do well if you really fulfill the royal law according to the scripture
Revelation 10:7	"the mystery of God will be fulfilled"
Revelation 11:7	When they have finished their testimony
Revelation 15:1	for with them the wrath of God is ended
Revelation 15:8	until the seven plagues of the seven angels were ended
Revelation 17:17	until the words of God will be fulfilled
Revelation 20:3	until the thousand years were ended
Revelation 20:5	until the thousand years were ended
Revelation 20:7	When the thousand years are ended
Matthew 17:24	"Does your teacher not pay [complete] the temple tax?"
Romans 13:6	For the same reason you also pay [complete] taxes
2 Corinthians 12:9	"My grace is sufficient for you, for power is made perfect in weakness"

Does not that last translation seem erroneous, in light of all the preceding usages? Certainly this list suggests that, though the verb *teleō* is obviously rich in nuances, it is indeed quite consistent in always being employed to indicate some sort of finishing, completing, ending, or accomplishing — rather than the perfecting or maturing of the verb *teleioō*. Why should 2 Corinthians 12:9, then, be translated as if the verb there were *teleioō*? It seems that the practice is so entrenched that scholars have a difficult time imagining an alternative.

For the rest of this chapter we will assume that 2 Corinthians 12:9 should be translated with the sense of "ending." What are the advantages to be gained from rendering the verb *teleō* in this way?

It seems to me that to do so makes more sense of the relationship of human weakness to God's power. See how you respond to this translation of Paul's description in 2 Corinthians 11:30 and 12:7-10:

> If it is necessary to continue boasting, I will boast of those things which show my weaknesses. . . . Therefore, to keep me from being too elated, a thorn in the flesh was given to me, a messenger of Satan to knock me about, to keep me from being too elated. Three times I appealed to the Lord concerning this, that it might depart from me, but he said to me, "My grace is sufficient for you, for [your] power is brought to its end in weakness." All the more gladly, then, will I boast in my weaknesses that the power of Christ [not mine!] may tabernacle upon me. Therefore, I take delight in weaknesses, in insults, in necessities, in persecutions and calamities for the sake of Christ, for when I am weak, then I am strong.

The goal is for our power to come to its end. But why?

Weakness and the Tabernacling of God

The possibilities for a refreshing theology of weakness are amplified when we recognize that the verb translated "dwell" in the NRSV rendition of 2 Corinthians 12:9 is actually *episkēnoō* or "to tabernacle." Louw's and Nida's *Greek-English Lexicon of the New Testament Based on Semantic Domains* lists about twenty different Greek verbs that signify "remaining/staying" or "dwelling/residing" somewhere.[5] Why, from this large domain,

---

5. See Louw and Nida, eds., *Greek-English Lexicon of the New Testament Based on Semantic Domains*, vol. 2, domains 85C and E, pp. 729-33.

might Paul have chosen to employ *episkénoō*, which is used only here in the New Testament, to describe the source of his contentment, even delight, in weaknesses?

The root of this Greek verb even sounds like the related First Testament verb (שָׁכַן, *shkn*), "to dwell." The first use of this latter verb in the Hebrew canon is found in Exodus 24:16: "The glory of the LORD *dwelt* on Mount Sinai, and the cloud covered it for six days." (Later this verb developed into the technical term, *shekinah*, for God's presence.) The verb is next employed in Exodus 25:8 — "And have them make me a sanctuary, so that I may dwell among them" — in which the word translated "sanctuary" signifies the "holy place" and is used later to name the Temple. In the following verse, Exodus 25:9, and throughout the rest of Exodus, the word *mishekan* ("dwelling," "tabernacle," derived from the root *shkn*) specifies the structure that is being made and erected. This noun occurs 140 times in 130 verses. The significance of the tabernacle for the life of Israel is suggested by the canonical choice to include thirteen chapters in Exodus describing it, in contrast to only three chapters for the accounts of the creation and fall.

Exodus 29:45 concludes with this strong reason why Israel was brought out of Egypt: so that *YHWH* could live/dwell among them and be their God. The verb is used both in verse 45 and again in verse 46: "And they shall know that I am the LORD their God, who brought them out of the land of Egypt that I might dwell among them; I am the LORD their God." The verb occurs one final time in Exodus in the dramatic account of 40:35 that "Moses was not able to enter the tent of meeting because the cloud settled [literally, tabernacled] upon it, and the glory of the LORD filled the tabernacle."

When *shkn* was first employed in Exodus 24:16, it declared that the glory of *YHWH* settled down or dwelt on the mountain and the cloud covered it. In 40:35 the cloud dwells/settles down on the tent of meeting. *YHWH* had announced that the purpose of the sanctuary was for Israel's LORD to dwell with them and be their God; now they had visible proof that this was so. The continuity between the two places, Mt. Sinai and the tabernacle, suggests a continuing revelation of God's will and presence.

In fact, a form of the same verb, *shkn*, is used in 1 Kings 6:13 when the Temple is dedicated. God promises: "I will dwell among the children of Israel and will not forsake my people Israel." That promise is repeated in Ezekiel 37:27 in noun form: "My dwelling place shall be with them; and I will be their God, and they shall be my people." All of this First Testament emphasis on God's "tabernacling" would have been in the back of the minds of the Jewish New Testament authors.

Their writings use the Greek noun *skēnē*, which sounds similar to *shkn*, twenty times for "tent" or "tabernacle." Three of these usages are in connection with Jesus' transfiguration (Matt. 17:4; Mark 9:5; Luke 9:33), and once Luke refers to dwellings that are eternal (Luke 16:9). The noun is also employed often in Hebrews to discuss the tabernacle (8:2, 5; 9:2-3, 6, 8, 11, 21; 13:10) and once to designate the "tents" in which Abraham dwelt (11:9). These occurrences of the noun in connection with Jesus (especially as the great High Priest) show us how the Hebrew idea of God's presence was "in the air" at the time the New Testament was written.

Indeed, the Greek noun *skēnē* had been utilized about 435 times in the Septuagint to translate the Hebrew word for "tabernacle." Because of developments in the Hebrew faith, the idea of "tabernacle" began to lose the sense of transitoriness associated with the tent that it had been in the wilderness and to become more often used figuratively or poetically to indicate God's dwelling — not that God lives in a tent, but that God dwells in the heavenly pattern after which the earthly tabernacle was modeled. This is the idea developed so carefully in the New Testament letter to the Hebrews.

For that reason, it is a delight to discover how the verb *skēnoō*, "to pitch a tent" or "to dwell in a tent," occurs in the New Testament. The first use of the verb is in John 1:14, "The Word became flesh and made his dwelling ["tabernacled," *eskēnosen*] among us. We have seen his glory, the glory of the One and Only, who came from the Father, full of grace and truth." This magnificent statement of the incarnation is all the richer when we connect it to the First Testament promises of God's dwelling with us and being our God.

The other four uses of *skēnoō* are in Revelation, along with several appearances of the noun *skēnē*. Most important for our purposes are these:

Revelation 7:15   "Therefore, they are before the throne of God,/and worship him day and night within his temple;/and the one who is seated on the throne will shelter [tabernacle over] them."

Revelation 21:3   And I heard a loud voice from the throne saying, "See, the home [tabernacle] of God is among mortals. He will dwell [tabernacle] with them as their God; they will be his peoples, and God himself will be with them."

Of course, it is immediately obvious that the latter text reiterates the First Testament promises connected also with the tabernacle and Temple. What a sublime theme interlocking the entire meta-narrative from Exodus, through the entire First Testament, the Gospel of John, and Hebrews, to the final promises in Revelation!

Five other verbs from the root *skēnoō* grace the New Testament, of which three are forms employed in the Synoptics to record Jesus' words about the birds of the air "making nests" in the mustard shrub's branches (in Matt. 13:32; Mark 4:32; Luke 13:19) and one is used in Acts 2:26 to translate Peter's quotation from Psalm 34, "my flesh will live [perhaps 'nest'?] in hope." This verb *kataskēnoō* is used in the Septuagint to translate the Hebrew verb *shkn* in this promise from Zechariah: "Sing and rejoice, O daughter Zion! For lo, I will come and *dwell* in your midst, says the LORD. Many nations shall join themselves to the LORD on that day, and shall be my people; and I will *dwell* in your midst" (2:10-11).

The remaining verb from the root *skēnoō* is simply stunning! Why would Paul choose *episkēnoō* in 2 Corinthians 12:9 to describe God's power coming to dwell with us in our weakness? We can't even be sure how the verb should be translated, for it occurs nowhere else in the New Testament, nor in the Septuagint, Philo, or Josephus.

Tabernacling and Ending of Power

Perhaps a key lies in looking more closely at God's past, present, and future tabernacling. In the context of the New Testament books in which the "tabernacling" verbs occur, it is also interesting that all the uses of *skēnoō* related to God are accompanied by forms of *teleō* and not *teleioō*. In the Gospel of John, Jesus tabernacled among human beings (1:14) and later completed his work with the cry recorded by the narrator as *tetelestai* ("It is finished," the same word printed on a prisoner's cell when the debt had been paid in full). Similarly, as we noticed in the sets of texts above, in the book of Revelation God tabernacles among human beings at the *telos* or end of things. Eight times in Revelation the verb *teleō* refers to occasions when various dimensions of the final days are brought to their completion. Thus, if we properly translate *teleō* instead of *teleioō* in 2 Corinthians 12:9, we see that Paul's power is brought to its end in his weakness; consequently, Paul glories in his weakness because through its very existence

Christ is able to reveal his presence with him (Christ's power tabernacles on him) in a unique way.

Thus, verses 9 and 10 together present this key progression: in verse 9a, Paul is weak with his power ended; in verse 9b, therefore Christ's power tabernacles on him; consequently, in verse 10, though Paul is weak, he is strong because of Christ's power in him and through him.

This is similar to the progressions constantly sketched throughout the New Testament and elucidated clearly in these words from Paul: "For through the law I died to the law, so that I might live to God. I have been crucified with Christ; and it is no longer I who live, but it is Christ who lives in me" (Gal. 2:19-20). Dying to the law, dying to our selves, dying to our attempts to use our own power to accomplish God's purposes are all part of the gospel of grace — the end of ourselves and therefore the possibilities of new life with Christ, in vital union with him.

This interpretation is underscored by Paul's consistent use of "weakness" images in 1 and 2 Corinthians. Look carefully at this set of passages calling us to see God's methods of foolishness and weakness and to choose the same death to human wisdom, status, wealth, and power. You already know these texts well, but let their message concerning God's methods sink in deeply:

> For the message about the cross is foolishness to those who are perishing, but to us who are being saved it is the power of God. For it is written, "I will destroy the wisdom of the wise, and the discernment of the discerning I will thwart." Where is the one who is wise? Where is the scribe? Where is the debater of this age? Has not God made foolish the wisdom of the world? For since, in the wisdom of God, the world did not know God through wisdom, God decided, through the foolishness of our proclamation, to save those who believe. For Jews demand signs and Greeks desire wisdom, but we proclaim Christ crucified, a stumbling block to Jews and foolishness to Gentiles, but to those who are the called, both Jews and Greeks, Christ the power of God and the wisdom of God. For God's foolishness is wiser than human wisdom, and God's weakness is stronger than human strength.
>
> Consider your own call, brothers and sisters: not many of you were wise by human standards, not many were powerful, not many were of noble birth. But God chose what is foolish in the world to

shame the wise; God chose what is weak in the world to shame the strong; God chose what is low and despised in the world, things that are not, to reduce to nothing things that are, so that no one might boast in the presence of God. He is the source of your life in Christ Jesus, who became for us wisdom from God, and righteousness and sanctification and redemption, in order that, as it is written, "Let the one who boasts, boast in the Lord."

When I came to you, brothers and sisters, I did not come proclaiming the mystery of God to you in lofty words or wisdom. For I decided to know nothing among you except Jesus Christ, and him crucified. And I came to you in weakness and in fear and in much trembling. My speech and my proclamation were not with plausible words of wisdom, but with a demonstration of the Spirit and of power, so that your faith might rest not on human wisdom but on the power of God. (1 Cor. 1:18–2:5)

Do not deceive yourselves. If you think that you are wise in this age, you should become fools, so that you may become wise. (3:18)

On the contrary, the members of the body that seem to be weaker are indispensable. (12:22)

Last of all, as to one untimely born, he appeared also to me. For I am the least of the apostles, unfit to be called an apostle, because I persecuted the church of God. But by the grace of God I am what I am, and his grace toward me has not been in vain. (15:8-9)

We do not want you to be unaware, brothers and sisters, of the affliction we experienced in Asia; for we were so utterly, unbearably crushed that we despaired of life itself. Indeed, we felt that we had received the sentence of death so that we would rely not on ourselves but on God who raises the dead. He who rescued us from so deadly a peril will continue to rescue us; on him we have set our hope that he will rescue us again. (2 Cor. 1:8-10)

But we have this treasure in clay jars, so that it may be made clear that this extraordinary power belongs to God and does not come from us. We are afflicted in every way, but not crushed; perplexed, but not driven to despair; persecuted, but not forsaken; struck down, but not destroyed; always carrying in the body the death of Jesus, so that the life of Jesus may also be made visible in our bodies. For while we live, we are always being given up to death for Jesus' sake, so that the life of Jesus may be made visible in our mortal flesh. So death is at work in us, but life in you. (4:7-12)

For he was crucified in weakness, but lives by the power of God. For we are weak in him, but in dealing with you we will live with him by the power of God. (13:4)

My point in detailing these texts so thoroughly is so that we read all in a clump the full testimony to the Trinity's "hidden" way for working out God's purposes in the world. Even as Christ accomplished atonement for us by suffering and death,[6] so the Lord accomplishes witness to the world through our weakness. In fact, God has more need of our weakness than of our strength. Just as powers overstep their bounds and become gods, so our power becomes a rival to God. As the Psalms and Isaiah teach us, God's way is not to take us out of tribulations, but to comfort us in the midst of them[7] and to "exchange"[8] our strength in the face of them. By our union with Christ in the power of the Spirit in our weaknesses, we display God's glory.

Tabernacling

Lest we get too comfortable with this whole notion of God's tabernacling in our weakness, two cautions are in order. The first is to warn us that the

6. Very important perspectives on Christ's suffering, death, and work of atonement in light of the "scapegoat" theory of René Girard are offered in Willard M. Swartley, ed., *Violence Renounced: René Girard, Biblical Studies, and Peacemaking*, vol. 4 of *Studies in Peace and Scripture* (Telford, PA: Pandora Press U.S., 2000). This volume not only suggests aspects of Christ's willingness to be the scapegoat that parallel my emphasis on weakness, but also elaborates some excellent critiques of Girard's theory, especially when it is used to reduce the broad range of biblical images for atonement.

7. See Marva J. Dawn, *I'm Lonely, Lord — How Long? Meditations on the Psalms*, rev. ed. (Grand Rapids: Wm. B. Eerdmans Publishing Co., 1998).

8. See chapter 31 of Marva J. Dawn, *To Walk and Not Faint: A Month of Meditations on Isaiah 40*, rev. ed. (Grand Rapids: Wm. B. Eerdmans Publishing Co., 1997), pp. 182-89.

tabernacling of God is a bit terrifying if we really think about it. Remember this account in Exodus 3:1-15 when the LORD appeared to Moses in a flame of fire out of the midst of a bush:

> When the LORD saw that he turned aside to see, God called to him out of the bush, "Moses, Moses!" And he said, "Here am I." Then he said, "Do not come near; put off your shoes from your feet, for the place on which you are standing is holy ground." And he said, "I am the God of your father, the God of Abraham, the God of Isaac, and the God of Jacob." And Moses hid his face, for he was afraid to look at God. (vv. 4-6)

Jacob had reacted similarly in Genesis 28:16-17:

> Then Jacob woke from his sleep and said, "Surely the LORD is in this place — and I did not know it!" And he was afraid, and said, "How awesome is this place! This is none other than the house of God, and this is the gate of heaven."

Often the tabernacling of God arouses fear. How can we be so cavalier about God's presence? One of the results of theological movements that have reduced Jesus merely to someone after whom we model ourselves (see Chapter 3) is that we no longer think we have any need for biblical fear — and then we easily trivialize God. Why should we fear if there is no need for deliverance from ourselves?

The second caution arises from a possible interpretation of Paul's verb, *episkēnoō*, in 2 Corinthians 12:9. Why did Paul add the preposition *epi* to the verb? One possibility that suggests itself is that the addition connotes movement toward, but not arriving at. Thus Paul might be indicating that God's tabernacling can't be complete in this present time — that it awaits the full tabernacling portrayed in Revelation. Our human weakness is never total, so that we completely give up on our own power, although that is the goal. I know from repeated experiences that I never give up my feeble attempts totally; daily I need to die to my own renewed efforts to save myself.

This does not fill us with despair. We simply acknowledge our unending sinfulness — until Christ ultimately puts an end to it!

In the meanwhile, however, we know God's tabernacling more fully in other ways. Perhaps the most important tabernacling for Christians is in the eucharist. Berthold Von Schenk (1895-1974) describes that tabernacling this way:

> I can only confess what the Holy Eucharist means to me. Briefly it is this: That Christ gave Himself to be true Food of my supernatural life. Here I have the actual Presence and self-giving of the living Christ. He who gave Himself for me on the Cross is giving Himself to me as I come to the Altar. Then He gave Himself unto death. Now He gives Himself to me for life, that through His living Presence and Power He may do for me everything that His death has made possible for me. In the Holy Communion I have the greatest Realities. It is an unseen Presence, and yet in this unseen Presence there is no mere memorial, but the Birth, Life, Death, Resurrection, and Ascension brought down to today, space and time abolished.[9]

Other Biblical Texts on Weakness

As can be seen in the Corinthians texts above, biblical "weakness" is described not simply in that word, but in all the places where the New Testament writers show themselves as operating not out of their own skills, pedigree, background, training, or power, but out of their infirmities and dependency and humility. Frequently, the Scriptures picture the disciples or the Church with images not of power, but of smallness — or the work of God accomplished in the hiddenness of weakness.[10]

---

9. Berthold Von Schenk's *The Presence: An Approach to Holy Communion,* quoted in *For All the Saints: A Prayer Book for and by the Church,* vol. 1: Year 1, Advent to the Day of Pentecost, compiled and edited by Frederick J. Schumacher with Dorothy A. Zelenko (Delhi, NY: American Lutheran Publicity Bureau, 1994), p. 209.

10. Timothy B. Savage, in *Power Through Weakness: Paul's Understanding of the Christian Ministry in 2 Corinthians,* Society for New Testament Studies Monograph Series 86 (Cambridge: Cambridge University Press, 1996), p. 167, lists some of the most prominent texts in the Hebrew Scriptures: "Those who enjoyed the most dramatic manifestations of divine power were often those of the greatest humility" — men such as Abraham (Gen. 18:7), Moses (Exod. 3:11), Gideon (Judg. 6:15), and David (1 Sam. 18:23). "It is axiomatic in the OT that God 'dwells with the contrite and lowly of spirit' (Is. 57:15), 'looks to the humble' (66:22) and 'is near the broken hearted' (Ps. 34:18). Where there is humility there, too, will be the power of God."

If we are to understand properly how the Church can be true to its vocation as one of the powers in the world, we must see how pervasive this theme is. I will offer only a sampling here, a few illustrations from each book of the New Testament, so that we can see how suffused the Bible is with this emphasis. My purpose is to help us be clobbered with this painful question: Why are a large proportion of today's churches in North America not living out of weakness?

The New Testament begins in weakness when Matthew lists four foreign and/or violated women in the lineage of Jesus (Matt. 1:1-17) and hints at the danger Mary was in when Joseph thought about putting her away quietly (1:18-25).[11] "Blessed are the poor in spirit," the beatitudes begin — and they end by naming how blessed we are when we are reviled and persecuted and when others utter all kinds of evil things against us falsely on Christ's account (5:1-12).

That Jesus took our weaknesses upon himself is underscored in 8:17, when Matthew reminds us, "This was to fulfill what had been spoken through the prophet Isaiah, 'He took our infirmities and bore our diseases.'" The weakness of God's methods in contrast to the powers of the world (in this case political powers) is underscored by Pilate's guard sealing the tomb with the official Roman mark of authority (27:62-66) — thus making it actually illegal for Jesus to rise and come out of the tomb!

In the Gospel of Mark, weakness is demonstrated repeatedly in the "little people" of the narrative who always seem to demonstrate true faith in contrast to the Twelve. As David Rhoads and Donald Michie make clear in their literary study of Mark, the little people are the ones who illustrate Jesus' words about "losing one's life, renouncing oneself, and becoming least"; thus, they serve as a foil to the disciples, who don't seem ever to understand Jesus' way. Rhoads' and Michie's closing summary is a thorough description of what I mean by a theology of weakness:

> For in this world created by the author we have experienced the radical new order called for under God's rule, the possibilities of faith in God, the greatness of service for others, the destructiveness of dominating other people, the hidden power of redemptive suffering, the misuse of state and religion to achieve power and success, the poten-

11. See Beverly R. Gaventa, "He Comes as One Unknown," in "The Challenge of Christmas: Two Views," *Christian Century* 110, no. 36 (15 Dec. 1993): 1270-80.

tial blindness of religious commitment, the lure of a survivor mentality, the deep resistance to renouncing oneself and facing death squarely, the difficulty of choosing to be least, the courage of anonymous little people, the hardships of being faithful to the rule of God.[12]

Indeed, on the journey to Jerusalem Jesus declares that the disciples should identify with children if they want to participate in his kingdom (10:14-15). Most important, it seems that Mark is responding to objections to the way of the cross (weakness) when he includes Jesus' strongest rebuke — calling Peter "Satan" because he dismissed Jesus' description of his suffering (8:31-38). No doubt Peter wanted to prevent that suffering because he knew he would have to follow his Messiah in that cross-bearing.

The Gospel of Luke, of course, has more stories of outcasts, women, foreigners, and others who are weak than the other Gospels, all the way to his more thorough account of the women remaining at the tomb at the end of the passion. Already in the first few chapters we are stunned by his accentuation on the character of these "little people," correlative to Jesus' own. We cannot help but notice the humility, obedience, and thoughtful pondering of Mary in 1:26-56, particularly in contrast to Zechariah (see especially 1:18). Correspondingly, we ought not to let romanticized views of Christmas distract us from the realization that the shepherds chosen to be the first messengers of the Savior's birth were social outcasts (2:16-20) and that Jesus' parents brought to the Temple the offering of poor persons (2:22-24; see Lev. 12:8).

When we pause to think about the parables and stories of Jesus, we are struck by the fact that they are completely upside down from the point of view of the world's powers. Tax collectors are the righteous (Luke 18:9-14); a foreigner rather than religious leaders illustrates neighborliness (Luke 10:25-37); birds and lilies are more glorious than human splendor and achievement (Matt. 6:26-34); the tiniest seed becomes the haven of birds (Matt. 13:31-32); slaves are given an enormous trust by their master (Matt. 25:14-30); poor Lazarus rests on Abraham's bosom (Luke 16:19-31); the rich lose all they've amassed (Luke 12:13-21); the good shepherd lays down his life for his sheep (John 10:1-18). Lest we think these are stories just like the fairy tales where persons of heroic character but simple means win in

---

12. David Rhoads and Donald Michie, *Mark as Story: An Introduction to the Narrative of a Gospel* (Philadelphia: Fortress Press, 1982), p. 142.

the end, Jesus throws in the occasional tale in which a rascal is lifted up as a good model because he trusted in his master's grace (Luke 16:1-13).[13] The whole point of our weakness is the *gracious* tabernacling of God!

In the Gospel of John, we are warned that our fruitfulness hinges on our dependency on Christ's tabernacling when Jesus says, "Abide in me as I abide in you. Just as the branch cannot bear fruit by itself unless it abides in the vine, neither can you unless you abide in me" (15:4). John the Baptizer sets the best model for us in relationship with Christ when he rejoices as the bridegroom's friend and declares, "He must increase, but I must decrease" (3:28-30). We are surprised by the results of the immensity of Jesus' grace enfolding an abused and rejected Samaritan woman and thereby setting her free to be the messenger of the kingdom to her town (4:1-42). In spite of his weakness in denial, Peter is still commissioned by his Lord to feed the sheep (21:15-19). As Bill Wylie Kellermann insists, "If he is thereby commissioned with pastoral authority, it is predicated *on his very weakness*. The issue here is grace and the freedom to follow Christ, even in death. Peter's pastoral work begins and ends there."[14]

The accounts of the early Christians in Acts make abundantly clear that their powerful witness to their community and neighbors arose out of their weakness. Peter can hardly believe that he's actually been delivered from prison (Acts 12:1-17); Paul testifies to Festus, Agrippa, and Bernice in chains (25:23–26:32). Peter and John have no silver and gold, but in Christ's name a lame man can leap to praise God (3:1-11). Though the lame man was probably not arrested or subpoenaed, he was standing in the courtroom the next day after the apostles' imprisonment (4:1-10). Bill Wylie Kellermann captures the astonishing witness from that man's weakness with this description:

> The authorities don't want him there. He is the living evidence and testimony they want suppressed. They wish him lame again. Apparently he has simply walked in and presented himself. He has come to stand beside the disciples. These officials must know him from his

13. See Kenneth E. Bailey, *Poet and Peasant* and *Through Peasant Eyes: A Literary-Cultural Approach to the Parables in Luke* (Grand Rapids: Wm. B. Eerdmans Publishing Co., 1983), pp. 86-118.

14. Bill Wylie Kellermann, *Seasons of Faith and Conscience: Kairos, Confession, Liturgy* (Maryknoll, NY: Orbis Books, 1991), p. 192 (emphasis his).

daily station at the gate. Some perhaps are friendly regulars with alms. Some are condescending, the averted eyes. Some hustle by pretending not to see, and others, worst of all, mark him truly invisible.

They see him now. It must take incredible nerve to stand before them. This is a real transformation. It is a complete healing, body and soul and social relationship. The real miracle is not just that he's standing, but that he's standing there.[15]

Similarly, Paul stands "not ashamed" of the gospel in Romans (1:16-17), though some might think the weakness of Christianity might be a source of shame. Later he admits that while we were helpless, while we were enemies, is the very time that, and condition for which, Christ died for us (5:6-11) and that we are rescued even though we are not capable of being or doing what we want (ch. 7). Even when we don't know how to pray because of our weakness, the Spirit helps us (8:26), and we are predestined to be conformed to the image of the Son (8:29) — including his suffering and weakness.

I'm sure it is profusely evident by now that a theology of weakness pervades the New Testament, but I will continue to pile up examples to insure that we get the point: there is something seriously wrong with our lives and churches if we are operating out of strength, rather than the weakness in which God tabernacles. Let us be sure to notice that the theme is in every book of the New Testament, though now I will outline the list more sketchily:

Galatians	Paul's announcement of the gospel came in physical infirmity (4:13); he is crucified with Christ (2:20) and wants to boast of nothing except Christ's cross, by which the world is crucified to him (6:14).
Ephesians	We are loved and made alive together with Christ, saved utterly and exhaustively by grace, even though we were dead in our sin (2:1-10); though Paul[16] is the very least of all the saints, yet grace was given him to bring to the Gentiles the news of Christ's boundless riches (3:8).

15. Wylie Kellermann, *Seasons of Faith and Conscience*, p. 195.

16. For this brief overview of texts, I will simply use the canonical ascriptions for the author of letters as shorthand to designate either the writer himself or literary practices.

Philippians
Imprisonment helps to spread the gospel (1:12-14); the community is urged not to live from selfish ambition or conceit, but rather to imitate Christ's emptying (2:1-10); Paul can be glad and rejoice even when he is being poured out as a libation and offering for others' faith (2:17-18); Paul's goal is to share in Christ's sufferings and to become like him in his death (3:10).

Colossians
Christ's servants can actually complete what is lacking in Christ's afflictions for the sake of the Church (1:24-26); declaring the mystery of Christ leads to prison (4:3).

1 Thessalonians
In spite of persecution the Holy Spirit inspires joy and witness (1:6-10); Paul had been shamefully treated and encountered great opposition (2:2).

2 Thessalonians
The saints have been steadfast and faithful in the midst of persecutions and afflictions (1:4); with toil and labor, Paul had to work night and day (3:8).

1 Timothy
Admitting the same toil and struggle (4:10), the apostle urges the rich not to be haughty or to set their hopes on riches, instead of God (6:17-19); Timothy is urged not to let any one discount him for his youth (4:12).

2 Timothy
Timothy is exhorted not to be ashamed, but to join Paul in suffering for the gospel (1:8-10; 2:3); the apostle suffers hardship, even to the point of being chained like a criminal (2:9).

Titus
Paul names himself a slave of God (1:1); the saints are reminded to be subject to the powers (3:1); they were saved not by anything they had done, but entirely by mercy (3:5).

Philemon
Onesimus the slave is a child to Paul (10), has been useless (11), but is to be welcomed for the sake of the imprisoned Paul (17-21).

James
The saints are urged to face trials with joy (1:2-4); the lowly

can boast in being raised up (1:9-10); with meekness they are to welcome the implanted word that has the power to save them (1:21); true religion is to care for orphans and widows (1:27), to recognize that God has chosen the poor to be rich in faith (2:5) and thus to welcome them (2:8-17); the humble are graced (4:6-10); the prophets provide examples of suffering and patience (5:7-11).

1 Peter	The people of the royal priesthood follow one rejected by mortals (2:4-10) and live as aliens and exiles (2:11); they follow in the steps of the one abused, wounded (2:23-25) — the one who suffered (3:18; 4:1, 12-14; 5:1); they should clothe themselves with humility (5:5-10).
2 Peter	No prophecy ever came by human will, but by the gift of the Holy Spirit (1:20-21); the saints wait for God's fulfillment, which is delayed because God is patient to save (3:11-15).
1 John	We deceive ourselves if we think we aren't weak with sin (1:8-9); we need Christ's atoning sacrifice (2:1-2); we are children of God, but what that is we do not yet know (3:1-2); love is revealed not by us, but by the atoning sacrifice of the Son (4:7-10).
Jude	It is Christ who keeps us from falling, makes us stand without blemish, offers mercy as we rest in God's love (21, 24).

Perhaps 2 and 3 John are the only letters without explicit images of weakness, though they are thoroughly imbued with openness to communal hospitality. Throughout the New Testament, then, we have seen a diversity of evidences for weakness as God's primary method, including the weakness of a suffering Messiah, the weakness of our sinfulness that necessitates a Savior from outside ourselves, the weakness we have relative to the powers of the world, and the priority for our communities of welcoming the weak.

Four books of the New Testament — 1 and 2 Corinthians cited above, Hebrews, and the Revelation — are the most pronounced in acknowledging or advocating weakness. Who can ignore this tremendous accounting in Hebrews 11?

And what more shall I say? For time would fail me to tell of Gideon, Barak, Samson, Jephthah, of David and Samuel and the prophets — who through faith . . . obtained promises, . . . won strength out of weakness. . . . Women received their dead by resurrection. Others were tortured, refusing to accept release, in order to obtain a better resurrection. Others suffered mocking and flogging, and even chains and imprisonment. They were stoned to death, they were sawn in two, they were killed by the sword; they went about in skins of sheep and goats, destitute, persecuted, tormented — of whom the world was not worthy. They wandered in deserts and mountains and in caves and holes in the ground.

Yet all these, though they were commended for their faith, did not receive what was promised, since God had provided something better so that they would not, apart from us, be made perfect.

Therefore, since we are surrounded by so great a cloud of witnesses, let us also lay aside every weight and the sin that clings so closely, and let us run with perseverance the race that is set before us, looking to Jesus the pioneer and perfecter of our faith, who for the sake of the joy that was set before him endured the cross, disregarding its shame, and has taken his seat at the right hand of the throne of God. (Heb. 11:32–12:2)

Moreover, more than the other epistles Hebrews underscores the weakness of Jesus, our High Priest (2:5-10, 14-18; 4:14-16; 5:1-10). The result of his example, the author urges, should be our hospitality to strangers and our concern for those in prison (13:1-3).

The book of Revelation, often misunderstood to be primarily a gruesome vision of the end times, is instead a tribute to Christ's Lordship in our weakness — to give hope to those Christians suffering persecution in the first century and thus to strengthen us in our own struggles.[17] The saints groaning and grieving under Roman brutality are assured of a future with the multitudes of "those who had been slaughtered for the word of God and for the testimony they had given" (6:9), those "who have come out of the great ordeal" and "have washed their robes and made them white in the blood of the Lamb" (7:14). Because their Lord is the Lamb

17. See Marva J. Dawn, *Joy in Our Weakness: A Gift of Hope from the Book of Revelation* (St. Louis: Concordia Publishing House, 1994).

who was slaughtered and now is "worthy . . . to receive power and wealth and wisdom and might and honor and glory and blessing" (ch. 5), the saints can persevere in their tribulation.

They can believe with the church at Smyrna that Christ knows their affliction and poverty, that they will be given the crown of life, that they will not be harmed by the second death (2:8-11). They can trust that, as the woman about to give birth was rescued from the jaws of the dragon and her child, Christ, was "taken to God and to his throne," so the Church, "our comrades . . . have conquered [the accuser] by the blood of the Lamb and by the word of their testimony, for they did not cling to life even in the face of death" (12:1-12).

Imitating Jesus

The Pauline texts about Jesus crucified in weakness and inviting us so to be crucified with him, the Petrine texts about following in the footsteps of Jesus, whose suffering has left us an example, and the Revelation texts urging perseverance in affliction all raise crucial questions for churches in our times. We must remember that what is true of Jesus, Peter, and Paul is no doubt also true for churches, since most of the Bible is written in plural and since the Scriptures repeatedly show that the way of God is through weakness. If the Church is most faithful to its true vocation as a created power through the weakness that gives way to God's tabernacling, then we must ask such questions as these:

> Why have we turned pastors into successful CEOs instead of shepherds for the weak?
>
> Why do we search for pastors who are handsome, sophisticated, charismatic — instead of models in suffering?
>
> Why do our churches adopt practices of business life and its achievement models?
>
> Why do we resort to gimmicks, or what Jacques Ellul calls Technique, instead of practicing an "unadulterated handling of the Word"?

We have seen how pervasive the imagery of weakness is. We have discovered that God specifically tabernacles in weakness. Now we must ask how we can avoid corporately acting as fallen powers overstepping the bounds of our true vocation.

Luke Timothy Johnson makes the same point when in two sections, "The Gospel and the Gospels" and "The Truth That Is in Jesus," he gives a succinct summary of who Jesus is for us to copy in our weakness.[18] He asks what the pattern and meaning of the New Testament texts are as they refer to Christ or life in Christ — as that is "embedded in the earliest Christian experience and memory," as that is "faithfully mirrored in the Gospel narratives" (152). Then he proceeds to show how "Jesus in Mark is the suffering Son of man" (153) and how, though "Matthew and Luke feel free to alter virtually every other aspect of Mark, . . . this image of the suffering One they do not alter in the least" (154), nor does any of the rest of the New Testament (155-66). Johnson concludes,

> When the witness of the New Testament is taken as a whole, a deep consistency can be detected beneath its surface diversity. The "real Jesus" is first of all the powerful, resurrected Lord whose transforming Spirit is active in the community. But *following Jesus is not a matter of the sort of power* that dominates others, nor of "already ruling" in the kingdom of God (I Cor. 4:8). It is instead a matter of transformation according to the pattern of the Messiah. The "real Jesus" is therefore also the one who through the Spirit replicates in the lives of believers faithful obedience to God and loving service to others. Everywhere in these writings the image of Jesus involves the tension-filled paradox of death and resurrection, suffering and glory. (166, emphasis added)

A Theology of Weakness: Honoring the Weak Among Us and In Us

On one of my weakest days — and the day before leaving for three weeks of teaching in Australia — I discovered, after fifteen months of trying to get a new leg brace, that my old one, too, was giving me sores. I had a new

---

18. Luke Timothy Johnson, *The Real Jesus: The Misguided Quest for the Historical Jesus and the Truth of the Traditional Gospels,* paperback edition (HarperSanFrancisco, 1997), pp. 151-58 and 158-65, respectively. Page references to this book in the following paragraphs will be given parenthetically in the text.

wound on my foot, which meant going back on crutches, which had been my recurrent companion for months. I couldn't help but ask, "How does God expect me to go on, when my life is always so hard?"

Some days I'm thoroughly exhausted from all the strain of trying to manage with arthritic hands, a crippled leg, a blind eye, a deaf ear, kidneys functioning around 17 percent, dead intestinal and stomach nerves resulting in no peristalsis, pain leftover from cancer and jaw surgeries, the imminent possibility of losing vision in my remaining eye, and now the possibility that the bone dropping from the fusion of my foot will continue generating sores that will eventually necessitate amputation. And that isn't the whole list. Does God really need me to be this weak?

Yes!

I believe that, though I don't understand it. Part of our human weakness is to recognize that the workings of God are "hidden," mysterious, beyond our human comprehension. In the midst of our unknowing, however, God comes afresh with new tabernacling.

Sometimes I think the Holy Spirit moves the bookmarks in my devotional books so that I am regularly reminded that Christ's power tabernacles in my weakness. On that day before leaving for Australia these were the morning prayers for Friday of the Week of Epiphany 1:

Opening Prayer

Thou wouldst have us ask of thee, O God, whatsoever we will. Above all else we ask of thee thyself, thou who hast never yet lost hope for any one of us, though thou knowest us altogether. Seal upon us the image of him whom we worship. Gather up all our doubts and uncertainties into the meaning which thou alone canst give to our lives. Make perfect in our weakness thy strength, and in the midst of all our anxiety bestow upon us that costly peace of thine which can be ours only as thy will becomes our will. In Jesus' name. Amen.[19]

Closing Prayer

Father almighty, . . . who delights in the worship of a contrite heart, grant us grace in this hour of worship to forswear the pride to which our hearts are prone, to remember that you have made us and not we

---

19. *For All the Saints,* pp. 238-39. Page references to this book in the rest of this chapter will be given parenthetically in the text.

ourselves, that you are the beginning and the end of our life. Grant us to know the limit of our knowledge that we may seek your wisdom and to know the limit of our power so that we may glory in your strength which is made perfect in weakness. So may we worship you in humility, and arise to newness of life by fellowship with you. Amen. [Reinhold Niebuhr (1892-1971)] (240)

To Help Us Rest in Our Weakness

I close this chapter simply with devotional prayers and thoughts because I know that we are not really glad to be weak. What will inspire us to accept the cross? What will enable us to give up our own efforts so that God can work through us? What will imbue us with humility to resist the world's methods of power and to receive God's power acting through us instead? What will help us not turn away from the suffering that might offer the very possibility for Christ's tabernacling power?

The rest of this chapter offers texts for further reflection if you want to spend time thinking about this crucial aspect of our life in faith; I have simply recorded passages that came up in my devotional reading in the past few weeks. Feel free to set these aside for now if you want — and come back to these passages when you need reminders or comfort or hope — and skip to the last two paragraphs of this chapter.

A great woman of the last century, Mother Janet Stuart, was accustomed to say to her novices: "Think glorious thoughts of God — and serve Him with a quiet mind!" And it is surely a fact that the more glorious and more spacious our thoughts of Him are, the greater the quietude and confidence with which we do our detailed work will be. Not controversial thoughts, or dry academic thoughts, or anxious worried thoughts, or narrow conventional thoughts. All these bring contraction instead of expansion to our souls; and we all know that this inner sense of contraction or expansion is an unfailing test of our spiritual state. We should have awed and delighted thoughts of a Reality and Holiness that is inconceivable to us, and yet that is Love. A Reality that pours itself out, in and through the simplest forms and happenings, and makes itself known under the homeliest symbols; that is completely present in and with us, determining us at every

moment of our lives. Such meditations as these keep our windows
open towards Eternity; and preserve us from that insidious pious
stuffiness which is the moth and rust of the dedicated life.

Evelyn Underhill (1875-1941)
in *Concerning the Inner Life* (in *For All the Saints,* 158)

I make myself nothing with Thee, Lord. I make Thee the entire sacrifice
of my pride, of the vanity which has possessed me up to the present.
Help my weak beginning. Keep from me the occasions of my falling.
"Turn my eyes that I see not vanity," that I see only Thee, and that I see
myself before Thee. It will be then that I shall know what I am and who
Thou art. Jesus Christ is born in a stable. He has to flee into Egypt. He
passes thirty years of His life in the shop of a craftsman. He suffers
hunger, thirst, weariness. He is poor, scorned, and abject. He teaches
the doctrine of heaven, and no one listens to Him. All the great and the
wise pursue Him, take Him, and make Him suffer frightful torments.
They treat Him like a slave, make Him die between two thieves, after
having preferred a thief to Him. That was the life that Jesus Christ
chose, and we, we have a horror of the slightest humiliation. Let us
compare our life to that of Jesus Christ. Let us remember that He is the
master, and we are the slaves. . . . Can we with justice feel contempt for
others and dwell on their faults, when we are full of them ourselves? Let
us commence to walk on the road which Jesus Christ has marked for
us, since it is the only one which can lead us to Him.

Francois de Salignac Fenelon (1651-1715)
from *Christian Perfection* (in *For All the Saints,* 356)

O God, the strength of all those who put their trust in you: Mercifully
accept our prayers; and because in our weakness we can do nothing
good without you, give us the help of your grace, that in keeping your
commandments we may please you both in will and deed; through
Jesus Christ our Lord, who lives and reigns with you and the Holy
Spirit, one God, for ever and ever. Amen.

Opening Prayer for Tuesday of the Week
of Epiphany 6 (in *For All the Saints,* 391)

Father of mercy. . . . By [your Son's] death and resurrection demolish
our pretensions of strength, and on the ruins build a temple worthy

61

of your name, so that all the world may know the glory of your transforming power, shown in Jesus Christ our Lord.

(in *For All the Saints*, 633)

Lord, dispel from us the error of pride and illusions of greatness, and
help us to abandon every vice and stand in awe of you, for you alone
are the Most High over all the world now and forever.

Prayer after Psalm 83 (in *For All the Saints*, 638)

The more confidence we have in our own strength and abilities, the
less we are likely to have in Christ. Our human weakness is no hin-
drance to God. In fact, as long as we do not use it as an excuse for sin,
it is good to be weak. But this acceptance of weakness is more than
acknowledging our limitations. It means experiencing a power much
greater than our own and surrendering to it. Eberhard Arnold, a
founder of the Bruderhofs, said, "This is the root of grace: the dis-
mantling of our power. Whenever even a little power rises up in us,
the Spirit and the authority of God will retreat to the corresponding
degree. In my estimation this is the single most important insight
with regard to the kingdom of God."

Johann Christoph Arnold[20]

The proud person always wants to do the right thing, the great thing.
But because he wants to do it in his own strength, he is fighting not
with man, but with God.

Søren Kierkegaard (1813-1855)[21]

Therefore, don't be fooled. It may well be that with great decisions others will marvel at you. All the same, you miss the one thing that is need-
ful. You may be honored in this life, remembered by monuments set up
in your honor, but God will say to you: "You unhappy person. Why did
you not choose the better path? Confess your weakness and face it."

---

20. Johann Christoph Arnold, *Seeking Peace: Notes and Conversations Along the
Way* (Farmington, PA: The Plough Publishing House, 1998), pp. 51-52.

21. Søren Kierkegaard, *Eighteen Upbuilding Discourses for Self-Examination,* ed.
and trans. Howard V. Hong and Edna H. Hong (Princeton: Princeton University Press,
1990), as quoted in Charles E. Moore, ed., *Provocations: Spiritual Writings of Kierkegaard* (Farmington, PA: The Plough Publishing House, 1999), p. 5.

Perhaps just in this weakness God will meet you and come to your aid. This much is certain: the greatest thing each person can do is to give himself to God utterly and unconditionally — weaknesses, fears, and all. For God loves obedience more than good intentions or second-best offerings, which are all too often made under the guise of weakness.

Søren Kierkegaard[22]

So it is with dying to yourself and to the world. But then, my listener, remember that then comes the life-giving Spirit. When? When you are dead to everything else. When does the Comforter come? Not until you have died to your selfishness and come to the end of your own strength. Not until you in love to God have learned to hate yourself, even your ability, not until then can there be talk of the Spirit, of life, of *new* life.

Søren Kierkegaard[23]

As far as power is concerned, to rule the whole world with a scepter is nothing compared to ruling it with a reed — that is, by impotence — that is, divinely.

Søren Kierkegaard[24]

Just try to imagine that the Pattern is called a "Lamb." That alone is a scandal to the natural mind. Who has any desire to be a lamb?

Søren Kierkegaard[25]

You can worship only by becoming weak. Woe to the presumptuous person who in his proud strength is audacious enough to worship

22. Kierkegaard, *Eighteen Upbuilding Discourses*, as quoted in Moore, ed., *Provocations: Spiritual Writings of Kierkegaard*, p. 7.

23. Søren Kierkegaard, *Eighteen Upbuilding Discourses for Self-Examination* and *Judge for Yourself*, trans. Howard V. Hong and Edna H. Hong (Princeton: Princeton University Press, 1990), as quoted in Moore, ed., *Provocations: Spiritual Writings of Kierkegaard*, pp. 150-51.

24. Søren Kierkegaard, *The Journals of Søren Kierkegaard*, ed. and trans. Alexander Dru (London: Oxford University Press, 1938), as quoted in Moore, ed., *Provocations: Spiritual Writings of Kierkegaard*, p. 236.

25. T. H. Croxall, *Meditations from Kierkegaard* (London: James Nisbet and Company, LTD, 1955), as quoted in Moore, ed., *Provocations: Spiritual Writings of Kierkegaard*, p. 236.

God! The true God can be worshipped only in spirit and in truth — but precisely this is the truth that you are entirely weak. In fact, you are nothing.

Søren Kierkegaard[26]

Oh God, even though I am very little before you, this little — this being nothing before thee — is for me infinitely much. All else is to me worth nothing, absolutely nothing!

Søren Kierkegaard[27]

At every turn it appears an absurd mismatch: a woman and a dragon, a babe and the kings of this world, a messiah of utter folly and the power of death. But that is precisely the method that God has chosen in the incarnation. God risks everything on the power of powerlessness. The topic of Christmas is whether we have the eyes to see it. And the heart to follow.

It is said in Revelation 12 that the woman and the dragon appear as a great sign. The Greek word is *semeion*. It's the same word the old prophet uses when he announces to Mary, "Behold, this child is set for the fall and rising of many in Israel and for a sign that is spoken against" (Luke 2:34). And it's the same word the angel announces to the shepherds, "And this will be a sign for you: you will find a babe wrapped in swaddling clothes and lying in a manger" (Luke 2:12).

John's preface holds that when the Word became flesh, many didn't recognize it. He was in the world, and the world was made through him, but it didn't know him. He came to his own, and they didn't acknowledge or receive him. But some did. Christmas has to do with seeing the signs, with recognition, with discerning God's presence in the world.

Bill Wylie Kellermann, considering
Revelation 12:1-9, 13-17 as a Christmas text[28]

---

26. Søren Kierkegaard, *Christian Discourses*, trans. Walter Lowrie (London: Oxford University Press, 1952), p. 137, as quoted in Moore, ed., *Provocations: Spiritual Writings of Kierkegaard*, pp. 411-12.

27. Croxall, *Meditations from Kierkegaard*, p. 55, as quoted in Moore, ed., *Provocations: Spiritual Writings of Kierkegaard*, p. 413.

28. Wylie Kellermann, *Seasons of Faith and Conscience*, p. 147.

In week five [of Lent], death is no longer figurative but actual fact. Jesus visits the home of Lazarus, whom he has raised from the dead, and there Mary anoints him for his own burial. His death is inevitable, which is the chief terror of the gospel. Here is the best man God ever made, who has done nothing but right all his life, and what is his reward? Not ripe old age with grandchildren hanging on his sleeve but early violent death on a cross. This death ruins all our efforts to turn the Bible into a manual for The Good Life. No one who has heard the story of Jesus Christ can mistake where following him will lead, which makes the gospel itself a text of terror for all who wish to avoid suffering and death. The Good News of God in Christ is heard loudest and best by those who stand on the far side of their own fresh graves.

On Palm Sunday we go through Luke's account of Christ's death in excruciating detail, as we will go through it again with John on Good Friday, but in between those two tombstones death recedes, looming above the narratives of Holy Week like a vulture in a tree. . . .

. . . In the background, the Old Testament lessons play the servant songs of Isaiah, reminding us that suffering has always been the vocation of God's chosen ones.

On Good Friday there is no escape. The vultures are perched low now; friends have vanished and the enemy is everywhere. The only good news is that there is one man who does not dissemble, one man who continues to speak the truth although it brings all the empires of this world crashing down on his head. According to John Jesus does not give up his ghost until he knows that "It is finished" (19:30). Whether or not he knows what happens next, he knows that he is part of something beyond himself, something he has brought to fullness by surrendering himself to it as to the incalculable, incomparable will of God.

In faith, we believe that the terrors of Lent and of our lives are purifying terrors, confounding clauses in a covenant we may nonetheless trust. While they are washing all our certainties away, it is hard to believe they may also be cleansing us of our illusions, but that is the dare. If we are tempted to draw back from it and seek an easier way, we are not alone. The world is full of former disciples. "Do you also wish to go away?" Jesus asks the handful who are left him in the sixth chapter of John (6:67). "Lord," Simon Peter answers him, "to whom can we go? You have the words of eternal life."

Barbara Brown Taylor, on preaching in Lent[29]

According to [John of] Ruysbroeck, we can also invite the presence of Jesus into our lives by cultivating a sense of our own destitution without him. In so doing we create what he calls a valley of humility. Of course, attaining genuine humility is not easy. We are prone in our fallen nature to find security in the pretense of our own strengths. Our culture tells us that it is the self-reliant and self-confident who prosper. Many of us have been raised in the "age of self-esteem." In fact, these self-building strategies bring death to our souls. . . .

It may be helpful to remind ourselves that at his first coming Jesus came not to the high and mighty, but to pious God-fearing folk of the countryside. Mary received Jesus into her life as a humble handmaiden of the Lord. . . . In the Sermon on the Mount, Jesus informs us that it is only the poor in spirit, the meek and the mourners, who will see the kingdom of God (and its King) break into their lives. Ruysbroeck tells us that the one who wants to practice the presence of Jesus needs to "take his stand upon his own littleness. . . . [He] confesses and knows that he has nothing, and is nothing, . . . and when he sees how often he fails in virtues and good works, then he confesses his poverty and his helplessness."

Mark Harris, quoting John of Ruysbroeck[30]

Lord, High and Holy, Meek and Lowly,
Thou hast brought me to the Valley of Vision
   where I live in the depths but see Thee in the heights;
   hemmed in by mountains of sin I behold Thy glory.
Let me learn by paradox that the way down is the way up,

---

29. Barbara Brown Taylor, "Preaching the Terrors," in *Exilic Preaching: Testimony for Christian Exiles in an Increasingly Hostile Culture*, ed. Erskine Clarke (Harrisburg, PA: Trinity Press International, 1998), pp. 89-90.

30. John of Ruysbroeck, *The Adornment of the Spiritual Marriage*, trans. C. A. Wynschenk (London: J. M. Dent, 1916), p. 18, quoted in Mark Harris, *Companions for Your Spiritual Journey: Discovering the Disciplines of the Saints* (Downers Grove, IL: InterVarsity Press, 1999), pp. 37-38.

that to be low is to be high,
that the broken heart is the healed heart,
that the contrite spirit is the rejoicing spirit,
that the repenting soul is the victorious soul,
that to have nothing is to possess all,
that to bear the cross is to wear the crown,
that to give is to receive,
that the valley is the place of vision.
Lord, in the daytime stars can be seen from deepest wells,
and the deeper the wells the brighter Thy stars shine.
Let me find Thy light in my darkness,
Thy life in my death,
Thy joy in my sorrow,
Thy grace in my sin,
Thy riches in my poverty,
Thy glory in my valley.

Prayer of an anonymous Puritan

People are like stained glass windows; they sparkle and shine when the sun is out, but when the darkness sets in their true beauty is revealed only if there is a Light within.

Elisabeth Kubler-Ross, source unknown

Neither the accumulated wisdom of all the earth and the skies, nor languages, the Church Fathers, and daily reading of the Holy Scripture, nor immense learning and eloquence make a good theologian or pastor if the cross is not added. Through the cross God purifies, cleanses, strengthens, and perfects the light of His true knowledge, of true faith in Christ, of true understanding of the divine promises, proper prayer, hope, humility, and all the virtues which He has first planted in the heart through the Word. Those are secure spirits rather than real Christians who live each day happily and joyfully, thinking that when they read the lament of an Ezekiel, the prayer of a Jonah, and other Psalms, they are hearing only empty words and vain dreams; therefore they can neither understand these descriptions of a faith struggling under the heaviest of trials nor can they speak of them to others. Accordingly we should equip ourselves for the Cross, which is just as necessary for those who wish to serve the Church as air and food are for the maintenance of the body. . . . How can a person be able to understand the Gospel or teach it to others if he himself has not experienced the power of the Gospel in the midst of sorrows and trials?

David Chytraeus (1531-1600),
"A Meditation on the Cross"
(in *For All the Saints*, 989-90)

Can that sinner be turned into a saint? Can that twisted life be put right? There is only one answer: "O Lord, Thou knowest, I don't." Never trample in with religious common sense and say — "Oh, yes, with a little more Bible reading and devotion and prayer, I see how it can be done."

It is much easier to do something than to trust in God; we mistake panic for inspiration. That is why there are so few fellow workers with God and so many workers for Him. We would far rather work for God than believe in Him. Am I quite sure that God will do what I cannot do? I despair of [people] in the degree in which I have never realized that God has done anything for me. Is my experience such a wonderful realization of God's power and might that I can never despair of anyone I see? Have I had any spiritual work done in me at all? The degree of panic is the degree of the lack of personal spiritual experience.

Oswald Chambers (1874-1917),
My Utmost for His Highest (in *For All the Saints*, 1002)

[Screwtape, a senior devil, writes his nephew, Wormwood, a devil in training:]

You must have often wondered why the Enemy [God] does not make more use of His power to be sensibly present to human souls in any degree He chooses and at any moment. But you now see that the Irresistible and the Indisputable are the two weapons which the very nature of His scheme forbids Him to use. Merely to override a human will (as His felt presence in any but the faintest and most mitigated degree would certainly do) would be for Him useless. He cannot ravish. He can only woo. For His ignoble idea is to eat the cake and have it; the creatures are to be one with Him, but yet themselves; merely to cancel them, or assimilate them, will not serve. He is prepared to do a little overriding at the beginning. He will set them off with communications of His presence which, though faint, seem great to them, with emotional sweetness, and easy conquest over temptation. But He never allows this state of affairs to last long. Sooner or later He withdraws, if not in fact, at least from their conscious experience, all those supports and incentives. He leaves the creature to stand up on its own legs — to carry out from the will alone duties which have lost all relish. It is during such trough periods, much more than during the peak periods, that it is growing into the sort of creature He wants it to be. Hence the prayers offered in the state of dryness are those which please Him best. We can drag our patients along by continual tempting, because we design them only for the table, and the more their will is interfered with, the better. He cannot "tempt" to virtue as we do to vice. He wants them to learn to walk and must therefore take away His hand; and if only the will to walk is really there He is pleased even with their stumbles. Do not be deceived, Wormwood. Our cause is never more in danger than when a human, no longer desiring, but still intending, to do our Enemy's will, looks round upon a universe from which every trace of Him seems to have vanished, and asks why he has been forsaken, and still obeys.

C. S. Lewis (1898-1963),
The Screwtape Letters (in *For All the Saints,* 1042-43)

Two themes came to preoccupy my thoughts. First, the conviction that no man can do properly what he is called upon to do in this life unless he can learn to forget his ego and act as an instrument of God. Second, that for him personally the way to which he was called would lead to the Cross, i.e., to suffering, worldly humiliation, and the physical sacrifice of his life.

Dag Hammarskjöld (1905-1961),
Markings (in *For All the Saints,* 1146)

[The Journalist writes of himself in the third person:]

Brooding on this macabre harlequinade of power, more evident in the USSR even than in India under the British Raj, the Journalist turns his attention to another scene — Jesus in the wilderness being offered the kingdoms of the world by the Devil in person, who claims to have them in his gift, and makes no other condition for handing them over than that Jesus should abandon God and worship him, the Devil! What an opportunity for anyone with Utopian expectations to close with this offer, set up a kingdom of heaven on earth, and live happily ever after! Jesus, however, turns the offer down, on the ground that worshiping the Devil can only have devilish consequences. As an alternative to the kingdoms of the world, He proclaims a kingdom not of this world, where pride gives place to humility, and the quest for power becomes a quest for love — all this, not just in words, but embodied in the great drama of the Incarnation.

Following this line of thought, the Journalist comes to grasp that the climax of Jesus's earthly ministry, His Crucifixion, amounted to a *reductio ad absurdum* of what the Devil has on offer — which is power. Likewise, Pilate's ironical billing of Jesus on the Cross as "King of the Jews" misfires in the light of Jesus's true destiny as "God's Almighty Word leaping down from Heaven out of His Royal Throne." Again, the mockery of the Roman soldiers misfires when they dress Jesus up in a scarlet robe, put a crown of thorns on His head, give Him a reed to hold in His hand as a sceptre, and then kneel down before Him in obeisance, chanting: "Hail, King of the Jews!" The soldiers are not, as they suppose, just ridiculing a poor, distrought and deluded man about to be crucified, but holding up to ridicule all who exercise power, thereby making power itself derisory, so that thenceforth thorns will be woven into every crown, and under every scarlet robe there will be stricken flesh.

Malcolm Muggeridge, *Confessions of a Twentieth Century Pilgrim*[31]

It is Holy Week as I finish polishing this chapter. What a time and season to contemplate weakness! Here we wonder at Jesus in the utter humility of riding on the colt of an ass, though rightly praised for being the one coming in the name of the LORD. We cringe at his submitting to the powers instead of using their methods for the sake of defeating them. We wail at

---

31. Malcolm Muggeridge, *Confessions of a Twentieth Century Pilgrim*, quoted in *For All the Saints: A Prayer Book for and by the Church*, vol. 2: Year 1, the Season after Pentecost, compiled and edited by Frederick J. Schumacher with Dorothy A. Zelenko (Delhi, NY: American Lutheran Publicity Bureau, 1995), pp. 890-91.

the open-eyed, non-drugged intensity of his suffering and death for the sake of others.[32]

How can we learn to rest in his grace, so that we can similarly give ourselves completely into God's hands for God's purposes to be fulfilled, and then know in our daily resurrections that the true power belongs to God? How can we more faithfully remember the theology of weakness, the theology of the cross, that is at the core of Christianity? Our churches act as fallen powers when they forget the cross at their center.

32. For extraordinary meditations on the passion, see Walter Wangerin, Jr., *Reliving the Passion: Meditations on the Suffering, Death, and Resurrection of Jesus as Recorded in Mark* (Grand Rapids: Zondervan Publishing House, 1992).

3 Churches Being, and Acting as, Fallen Powers

In the previous chapter I asked why our churches don't resemble the weakness of Jesus, of Paul, of the early Church. Part of the answer to that question will be found if we return to the subject of Chapter 1 — the principalities and powers. If all the created powers tend, in this fallen world, to overstep their bounds — and if the Church and its servants are called instead to weakness so that the power of God may tabernacle in us — then it is important for us to notice in what ways churches live as fallen powers or function out of the biblical *sarx* (flesh) instead of Spirit. For example, how is the churches' vocation of weakness violated when they are influenced by other powers?

On the day at Pittsburgh Theological Seminary that I gave the lecture that forms the basis of this chapter, my morning devotions included Jeremiah 3:6-19, assigned for Wednesday of the second week of Lent. (Once again it almost seems as if God moved the bookmarks since this text appointed for the day was strikingly appropriate for what I was thinking and doing.) In this passage Jeremiah reports that *YHWH* commanded him to notice the harlotry of Israel "on every high hill and under every green tree," by which she "polluted the land, committing adultery with stone and tree" (3:6, 9). In this chapter we will be asking with what powers churches commit adultery in our times.

In the same set of devotional readings came this warning from the 1500s:

No one who has studied the matter will deny that in the course of its entire history the fortunes of the Church on earth have been determined in such a way that its preservation from harm or its downfall have depended exclusively on its pastors and bishops. From the foundation of the world the Church has always maintained its strength and flourished when these have faithfully persevered in their mission with fortitude. And the contrary is also true, that things could not have gone any worse for the Church than when its pastors and bishops have allowed themselves to be corrupted by Satan and have been in one way or another ousted from their positions. So, to achieve his ends as quickly as possible, the devil's chief concern is to stalk pious pastors and their ministry tirelessly, directing all the might of his vile nature solely to corrupting them, since their fall will of necessity bring in its train the collapse of the Church.[1]

I would modify de Reina's comment slightly because we know biblically that the health of the Church does not depend "exclusively" on its leaders, but certainly their own spiritual robustness is the most prominent influence on true Christianity's well-being. That is why I think this book is necessary, so that pastors and other spiritual leaders pay closer attention to the kinds of powers that lead us astray — both from outside our churches and from within. In this chapter we will primarily notice some of the ways in which those powers work. Naming them, recognizing them, and being vigilant against them are crucial parts of our "standing" in opposition to them.

We begin with a few simple illustrations to quicken our awareness of the scope, subtlety, seduction, and strength of the powers' corruptions. Though Australian social commentator Hugh Mackay was not speaking from a particularly Christian perspective, this insight from his inventory of pressing cultural issues offers food for thought:

The truth is that the spiritual impulse and the sporting impulse coexist in most of us; they both have important messages for us, but they have almost nothing to say to each other. And that, in a way, signifies the tension that has Australian society in its grip at the end of the

---

1. Casiodoro de Reina (1520-1594), *Ecclesiam Christi*, trans. A. Gordon Kinder, quoted in *For All the Saints: A Prayer Book for and by the Church*, vol. 1: Year 1, Advent to the Day of Pentecost, compiled and edited by Frederick J. Schumacher with Dorothy A. Zelenko (Delhi, NY: American Lutheran Publicity Bureau, 1994), pp. 833-34.

century. Our sporting impulse encourages us to think about economic growth, or globalisation, or industrial relations reform, in terms of *winning;* our spiritual impulse drives us to think about equity, fairness and justice, and about the impact of our success on the poor, the disadvantaged, the marginalised. In a culture that almost deifies competition, the sporting urge prevails most of the time.[2]

Is the sporting urge prevailing in our churches? Why do conversations at the dinner tables of pastors' conferences seem to focus more on comparisons (competition?) with other churches than on creating justice for the poor?

I wonder if the very prominent concern about survival in churches is a sign of their fallenness. As Bill Stringfellow pointed out, "The principalities have great resilience . . . [they adapt their] means of dominating human beings to the sole morality which governs all demonic powers so long as they exist — survival."[3] Both the concern for "church growth" and the concern for survival (which sometimes are the same thing) lead to many of the tactics of fallen powers, such as competition, the overwhelming pressures on church leaders to be successful, reduction of the gospel for the sake of marketing, and so forth.

Furthermore, what happens to church leaders who act out of their power or out of the pressures of power instead of out of the weakness that receives God's tabernacling? Speaking of secular leaders, Stringfellow writes,

> In truth, the conspicuous moral fact about our generals, our industrialists, our scientists, our commercial and political leaders is that they are the most obvious and pathetic prisoners in American society. There is unleashed among the principalities in this society a ruthless, self-proliferating, all-consuming institutional process which assaults, dispirits, defeats, and destroys human life even among, and *primarily* among, those persons in positions of institutional leadership. They are left with titles but without effectual au-

2. Hugh Mackay, *Turning Point: Australians Choosing Their Future* (Sydney: Pan Macmillan Australia, 1999), pp. 234-35.

3. William Stringfellow, *An Ethic for Christians and Other Aliens in a Strange Land* (Waco, TX: Word Books, 1973), p. 93.

thority; with the trappings of power, but without command over the institutions they head; in nominal command, but bereft of dominion. These same principalities, as has been mentioned, threaten and defy and enslave human beings of other status in diverse ways, but the most poignant victim of the demonic in America today is the so-called leader.[4]

Isn't that an apt description of the way many pastors feel today? Just this morning I was engaged in conversation with a counselor who is working with a pastor enslaved by the need to keep up a wicked pace in order that the congregation he serves can continue "growing." Is a parish growing well if the pastor himself is too frantically busy to care for his own spiritual nurturing?

Bill Wylie Kellermann shows us the reason power makes victims of its wielders by looking to the biblical account of Jesus and the temptations. He observes that

The insidiousness of the temptations lies in the integrity of how and who. Power and person are the topic. The one crouched ready to gobble up the other. Power may consume, corrupt, inflate, distort, dissipate, or simply deaden the person. The Confuser's scheme is for Jesus to forget who he is by getting lost in how he'll work, so that the One who is the beginning and end will be swallowed up in the means.

It seems more and more widely recognized that each of the temptations is to power: the first is to economic power, the second is to military/political power, and the third is to religious power. In all, we're granted a concise and compact exchange on issues at once very concrete to the life of Jesus and pertinent to our own. Remember that at the conclusion of the encounter the tempter doesn't slink off into oblivion forever defeated; he withdraws "until an opportune time." Such times present themselves repeatedly to Jesus and his followers.[5]

Our times seem to be opportune for great temptations; consequently, my main purpose in this chapter is to rouse us to greater vigilance.

---

4. Stringfellow, *An Ethic for Christians*, pp. 88-89.
5. Bill Wylie Kellermann, *Seasons of Faith and Conscience: Kairos, Confession, Liturgy* (Maryknoll, NY: Orbis Books, 1991), pp. 159-60.

I don't think that we can overstate the danger of churches losing their vocation and functioning out of their fallenness. Wylie Kellermann calls Americans "hopelessly naive" concerning the "depth and ubiquity" of the fall. Especially for our purposes here it is essential that we realize how fallen we are, both as individuals and corporately.

Dorothy Day, co-founder with Peter Maurin of the Catholic Worker Movement, could be acerbic about churches under the influence of the world's powers, though throughout the years after her conversion she was a devout Catholic. Robert Coles reports from his extensive conversations with her that she frequently responded to a query with the devastating Romano Guardini quote, "The Church is the Cross on which Christ was crucified." Coles comments, "It clearly haunted her; I counted it in my tape scripts eleven times!" At other times "she called upon François Mauriac or Georges Bernanos for a similar attack from within. These two intensely loyal Catholic novelists had no illusions about the church's capacity to harbor the devil and multiply him into a legion of respected ecclesiastical functionaries."[6]

Have churches always had such a capacity? Was there ever a golden time when God's people were truly Church?[7]

It is common in theological circles to talk about the Constantinian Fall of the Church in the 300s, when the Holy Roman Catholic Church became aligned with the powers of the Roman state. This led, of course, to entirely new power configurations. Jacques Ellul also adds the major falls of churches when they compromised with capitalism in the nineteenth century or lost their revealed truth in adopting certain scientific methods in the same epoch.[8]

However, we must realize that Christians before and after these times

---

6. Robert Coles, *Dorothy Day: A Radical Devotion,* Radcliffe Biography Series (Reading, MA: Addison-Wesley Publishing Co./Perseus Books, 1987), pp. 66-67. See also these books by Georges Bernanos: *The Diary of a Country Priest,* trans. Pamela Morris (Garden City, NY: Doubleday and Company, [1937], 1954) and *The Heroic Face of Innocence: Three Stories by Georges Bernanos* (Grand Rapids: Wm. B. Eerdmans Publishing Co., 1999).

7. Keep in mind that in this book I am using capitalized *Church* to signify the ideal as Christ would have his Body be and uncapitalized *church* or *churches* to name concrete fallen (and seeking to be faithful) realities.

8. Jacques Ellul, *The Presence of the Kingdom,* trans. Olive Wyon (New York: Seabury Press, 1967), p. 152.

have always struggled with their personal and corporate fallenness. A great proportion of the New Testament was written to instruct, rebuke, correct, and exhort early Christians so that they would be more faithful in following the example of Jesus. Since it is a universal and constant problem that powers overstretch their limits, the question of this chapter must be how, in this particular time and culture, churches need to be vigilant against temptations to operate as a fallen power instead of according to our true vocation.

In Search of an Organizing Principle

It is easy to say that our churches are sinful. The problem is to find a means by which we can sketch the nature of our fallenness in these times, especially because we want to look particularly at the loss of our call to weakness instead of to power. Various positive biblical texts suggest themselves as organizing principles:

> Jesus' description of blessedness in the Beatitudes, Matthew 5:1-16;
> Paul's earliest instructions to the community in 1 Thessalonians 5:12-24 or his later instructions to the Romans in chapter 12;[9]
> the reminder in 1 Peter 2:9 that we are a "chosen race, a royal priesthood, a holy nation, God's own people, in order that [we] may proclaim the mighty acts of him who called [us] out of darkness into his marvelous light";
> portraits in Acts of the early Christians as the gospel began to spread.

It is good for us to ponder many texts in the New Testament to think about both what forms our fallenness takes (as we will consider in this chapter) and what our weakness might look like (as we will see in the next chapter). Finally, however, Luke's Greek particles *men* and *de* drew me to Acts 2 as an excellent vehicle for our investigation of our churches' straying from our true vocation. Those little words in Acts 2:41, signifying "on the one hand" and "on the other," knit together in an integral way the calling/saving power of the Lord with the devoted response of the early Christians.

9. For an intensive study of this text, see Marva J. Dawn, *Truly the Community: Romans 12 and How to Be the Church* (Grand Rapids: Wm. B. Eerdmans Publishing Co., 1992; reissued 1997).

The scene in Acts 2 is dramatic. The pouring out of the Spirit has caused bewilderment and astonishment in the city (2:6-7). In reply to the sneering and amazement (vv. 12-13), Peter has given his extraordinary account of the meta-narrative (the overarching story) of God's foretelling of the Messiah and its fulfillment in Jesus (vv. 14-36). The people are "cut to the heart" and urgently entreat the disciples, "what should we do?" (v. 37). Peter calls them to repentance and baptism, to the gifts of forgiveness and the Holy Spirit (v. 38). He assures everyone that God's promise is for them, for their children, for all, whether near or far (v. 39), but particularly he urges them, "Save yourselves from this corrupt generation" (v. 40).

The whole occasion is a startling combination of God's power and human weakness: the fire of the Spirit poured out in the power of courage and languages; the weakness of the disciples, not understanding how they could speak so forcefully and in divergent tongues; the dominion of God, whose "deeds of power" (v. 11) are the subject of their speech; the belittlement when the apostles are scoffed for being drunk; the sovereignty of God whose ancient promises are fulfilled; the weakness of Jesus (as narrated by Peter), who accomplished those sovereign purposes by being handed over to the crushing contradiction of crucifixion; the crowning glory that "the entire house of Israel [could] know *with certainty* that God has made him both Lord and Messiah, this Jesus whom [we] crucified" (v. 36); the humbled weakness of being "cut to the heart" (v. 37); the glorious power of forgiveness and Holy Spirit giftedness; the utter frailty of Christians in the midst of a corrupt generation (v. 40).

How, then, did they live in such a state? What was their posture right at the very beginning, in response to the powerful outpouring of the Holy Spirit? The particles *men* and *de* introduce the fused results: on the one hand, the Lord added a large number to the community; and, on the other — inextricably connected to the Lord's calling — they all lived ardent lives exhibiting certain characteristics. Their fidelity was constant as they continually devoted themselves (signified by the Greek phrase *ēsan proskarterountes*, in v. 42) to these seven practices:

1. the apostles' doctrine/teaching *(didachē)*
2. fellowship *(koinōnia)*
3. breaking of bread
4. prayers
5. many signs and wonders

6. being together, having all things in common, selling their property and possessions, distributing the proceeds to all as any had need
7. day by day, being devoted (cf. v. 42) with one mind in the temple praising God and also worshiping/breaking bread from house to house.

The results of this way of life were that the believers experienced gladness and simplicity/generosity/sincerity of hearts, God was praised, and they had the "goodwill of all the people" (vv. 46-47). The Church grew — not because of the power of these believers, but because "the Lord added to their number day by day those who were being saved" (v. 47b).

Of course, the first Christians weren't always faithful to this vision. The book of Acts reports many early examples of idolizing other powers, such as when money became mammon to Ananias and Sapphira (Acts 5). Let us keep in mind the vision of Acts 2, however, and use its outline to investigate how present churches have fallen away from these practices. How have we lost sight of this vision?

Of course, I am aware of the "dangers of hectoring, of finger wagging, an occupational hazard of all reformers."[10] However, together with all those who care passionately about the Church and want to see it (and all of us, its members) called to greater integrity, I can't help but write with the prayer that these pages will at least raise awareness and vigilance, as well as faithfulness and hope for pastors and spiritual leaders and congregations.

My concerns parallel those of Jacques Ellul when he wrote *False Presence of the Kingdom* in 1963. His comments are remarkably timely for our purposes here as we note ways in which churches act as fallen powers instead of faithfully fulfilling their vocation to praise God and serve human life. Ellul insisted that he wrote, not to condemn or in a spirit of superiority, but because "living by the very life of the Church, I feel myself affected by everything which looks to me like compromise or error." As Ellul asserts, "There is no passing of judgment on my brothers [or sisters]. It is purely a matter . . . of trying to see clearly."[11]

Thank God many people are working to clarify our sight! In the newest volume from the Gospel and Our Culture Network, Darrell Guder seeks to

10. This phrase is from Robert Coles, *Dorothy Day*, p. 88, describing Day's consciousness of those dangers.

11. Jacques Ellul, *False Presence of the Kingdom,* trans. C. Edward Hopkin (New York: Seabury Press, 1972), pp. 5-6.

spur *The Continuing Conversion of the Church*. He perceives that it is "a 'principalities and powers' question: the gospel is quickly reduced when confronted with questions of institutional power, wealth, and influence."[12] Let us turn, then, to those seven characteristics of the earliest Christians in order to discern some of the ways in which contemporary powers beguile us and lead us astray from those practices and from God. It is not possible to elaborate all the ways in which churches fall to the seductions of various powers; the rest of this chapter will simply sketch a few examples, with the hope that these will spur your own questions, your recognition of the specific temptations of your own situations.

Seven Practices of the Early Church

1. The Apostles' Teaching

Method

What was "the apostles' teaching," and why was it so important in the early Church? As we look at the sermons in Acts and the letters in the New Testament we notice that the apostles taught the First Testament Scriptures and Jesus Christ as the fulfillment of God's promises. Their primary message was that Jesus, who was crucified by all of us, is risen from the dead — and that this truth changes everything! We will look more closely at this content in the following section, but first it is essential that we consider the problems of method that reveal workings of the powers in our times.

As George Lindbeck makes clear, faith is not simply intellectual agreement with doctrinal propositions, nor expressions of generalized emotions; rather, it is a language that we continue to learn[13] — a "walking" of this truth of the resurrection. Doctrine is critical, Lindbeck notes, because it is the grammar of the language, the skeleton of the body of faith. Straight doctrine is essential, I want to add, because if the bones are bent, churches under pressure will snap at the point of crookedness.

12. Darrell L. Guder, *The Continuing Conversion of the Church*, The Gospel and Our Culture Series, gen. ed. Craig Van Gelder (Grand Rapids: Wm. B. Eerdmans Publishing Co., 2000), p. 194.

13. See George Lindbeck, *The Nature of Doctrine: Religion and Theology in a Postliberal Age* (Philadelphia: Westminster Press, 1984).

This portrait is graphically evident in my life. More than a dozen years ago, because of a misdiagnosis and various complications, I wound up with a shattered foot, which was rebuilt after a year in casts, but then my leg broke and healed with a bend in it. Consequently, for the past eleven years my left leg has been encased daily in a toe-to-knee plastic brace so that the bones won't break where the leg is bent. The brace becomes a handy illustration for the importance of straight doctrinal bones as the basis for the Body's fleshing out of the Christ-life.

For almost an entire year, including the time when I presented these Schaff Lectures at Pittsburgh Theological Seminary, I have had to be on crutches because of ulcerated wounds inside my leg brace, caused by deterioration of my foot and the attempts of four different orthotics makers to construct a new brace. My inability to walk and the resultant frustrations and exhaustions underscore powerfully that we cannot fix churches' crooked doctrinal bones merely by propping them up from the outside. Eventually those props lead to woundedness that hampers the congregation's ministries, even as the original crookedness unpropped leads to brokenness. Either way, we can't walk in true faith.

In *The Subversion of Christianity,* Jacques Ellul asks this basic question (one, he declares, that troubles him most deeply): "How has it come about that the development of Christianity and the church has given birth to a society, a civilization, a culture that are completely opposite to what we read in the Bible, to what is indisputably the text of the law, the prophets, Jesus, and Paul?"[14] He charges that Christian practice has constantly been a subversion of the truth in Christ, which includes "[f]irst, the revelation and work of God accomplished in Jesus Christ, second, the being of the church as the body of Christ, and third, the faith and life of Christians in truth and love" (11). He insists that if our Christianity were true in this way, it would itself actually be subversive of every other kind of power, including mammon, political power, religious phenomena, morality, and culture (13-18). In not subverting these powers but submitting to them instead, and in failing to let their own power be subverted by weakness, churches reject the tabernacling of God.

Ellul stresses that Christianity has been subverted because its true mes-

---

14. Jacques Ellul, *The Subversion of Christianity,* trans. Geoffrey W. Bromiley (Grand Rapids: Wm. B. Eerdmans Publishing Co., 1986), p. 3. Page references to this book in the following paragraphs will be given parenthetically in the text.

sage of grace is so difficult to live in all its dialectical tension (43). Ellul insists that *everything* in the Bible is contradictory,[15] but that "there is revelation only as the contradictions are held together" (44). Such contradictions as Luther's *"Semper simul peccator et justus"* ("always at the same time sinners and justified") and the fact that the Wholly Other could be incarnate as a man and still be the Wholly Other reveal the importance of recognizing that truth is made up of contradictions, the separation of which renders each part false and deceptive (44-45). It seems to me that the failure to capture the fullness of biblical dialectics is what leads to many of our problems with methods of doctrine in the churches.

When dialectical truths are not held in tension, one side or the other is easily sacralized. That is, one side is so divinized that the other side is lost. In the midst of his thorough explication of this theme of desacralization and sacralization (52-68), and with reference to the emphasis in Hebrews that the unique sacrifice of Jesus annuls all the religious powers of corrupted Judaism,[16] Ellul stresses the following:

> Finally, the mysterious powers of the world are definitively exorcized, eliminated, and vanquished. This is an essential theme. The world contains spiritual powers variously described as thrones, *exousiai*, and dominions, etc. Residing in the world, these powers hide in institutions, people, etc. But they have all been destroyed and extirpated by the death and resurrection of Jesus Christ. (60)

What was gained in Christ's desacralizing of the powers of religion, mammon, politics, etc., is lost again, Ellul grieves, when Christianity becomes subverted by the reintroduction of the religious powers defeated by Christ.

Similarly, often political powers, economic ideologies, or scientific methods disrupt doctrine — as they frequently do in denominational assemblies and in the methods of our scholarship. I don't mean that we

15. Ellul typically overstated his case to make his point when he thought that it was not well enough recognized, very much as Flannery O'Connor wrote what she admitted to be grotesque stories as a megaphone to those refusing to hear. It is the same problem already noted in this chapter: how do we help churches see what does not seem to be noticed?

16. Let me stress that true Judaism is also built on dialectically understood grace. God brings Israel out of Egypt and calls them to a way of life empowered by *YHWH*'s presence.

shouldn't have political and economic responses, or that we don't value scientific inquiry. But because we are members of Christ's Body, we must let his Word describe our world rather than vice versa. To let ideologies control our theological work is to be subverted by powers other than God. Ellul contends that there is "no purely scientific procedure" in exegesis, but rather a "choice of values" (118). Do our own choices of hermeneutical, homiletical, and ecclesiological methods as theologians, pastors, and church leaders produce results appropriate to the texts themselves, or are our methods immersed in economic or political ideologies?

For example, are our churches' goals set by slogans of the culture around us or by biblical texts? Do our congregational programs find their source in the way sociology defines the present "needs" of consumers (should that read "their wants"?) or from the Scriptures? What decides the doctrinal content of the worship service — one who is theologically trained or the results of a survey asking people what they want? How much are the doctrinal foundations of a parish's work recognized in the decisions of the church board or council?

For many years Jacques Ellul wrestled with this problem of adopting the methods of the culture around us as we seek to dispense the gifts of the Church. In his *False Presence of the Kingdom* he potently asks, "Given the fact that you are constantly immersed in this bath [of the world's methods, powers, . . .], what can being a Christian in it possibly mean?"[17] He outlines the problem thus:

> Christians who are conformed to the world introduce into the Church the value-judgments and concepts of the world. They believe in action. They want efficiency. They give first place to economics, and they think that all means are good. . . . They are defined by their sociological milieu. The Protestant thinks to adopt the means which the world employs. Since he finds those means useful in his profession, or in his leisure time, they stand so high in his estimation that he cannot see why he should not introduce them into the Church and make the things of the spirit dependent upon them.
>
> He never faces the problem of these means. . . . They are effective. Hence they are good. Since they are in a sanctified world and are ef-

---

17. Ellul, *False Presence of the Kingdom*, p. 47. Subsequent page references to this book will be given parenthetically in the text.

fective, why not make use of them in the Church? The criteria of his thinking as a Christian are so vague, and the demands of his faith are so "inward," that he is unaware of any contradiction between the world's means and the life of faith. (47-48)

When such conformity to our society's thinking is countenanced, in such "adapting, one imports into the faith the *'stoikeia,'* the rudiments of the world, against which we are expressly warned" in Galatians 4:3 and 9 and Colossians 2:6 and 20 (58).

Consider, for example, the power of the media, with which this book began. Luke Timothy Johnson is one who shows the dangers of this particularly significant power, which thoroughly disrupts our doctrinal methods. Commenting on the response to the original publication of his book *The Real Jesus*, which strongly critiques the Jesus Seminary, he explains that "the sound of my whistle has been caught up into the surrounding noise and orchestrated as part of a continuing media event." Johnson complains in the first paperback edition of the book that "an important subject had been routed through the media rather than through the church and the academy. I found myself co-opted by the same process, with the points in my argument increasingly reduced to the level of comments on personalities, or position-taking sound bites."[18]

He continues:

I was confirmed in my sense that the media is the wrong place for such discussions to occur, not only because of its inability to deal with substantive issues adequately, but because participation in the media's productions inevitably draws people away from their primary cultural involvements. The power of the media to entice participation in its own efforts is powerful, for who can resist the chance to appear as worthy of attention by the priests of the culture? Also strong is the media's capacity to intrude into and disrupt one's life. In my case, I cannot remember a semester when I felt more strongly that my students were not receiving my best efforts. Once again, I found

---

18. Luke Timothy Johnson, *The Real Jesus: The Misguided Quest for the Historical Jesus and the Truth of the Traditional Gospels*, paperback edition (HarperSanFrancisco, 1997), pp. vii-viii. Subsequent page references to this book in this section and the next will be given parenthetically in the text.

> myself ironically guilty of the criticism I make in chapter 3 [of *The Real Jesus*], that those who seek to influence public opinion do so at risk to the more fundamental and important transformation of minds by teaching. (viii)

Similarly, we can note the dangers of the media to the important tasks of preaching or the work of pastoral ministry or congregational leadership. How much does it change the methods of our doctrine, our teaching, our way of life if we are attempting to influence public opinion, if we become ensnared in the *stoikeia* of the media? Similarly, some of our methods of biblical interpretation inevitably draw us away from our involvement in the Church. As Johnson protests, "The ways in which the historical-critical method have run amok are not disconnected from the ways in which biblical scholarship has become detached from communities for whom the writings of the Old and New Testaments have existential and normative importance" (ix).

If doctrine enters the "sound-bite" world of the media, how much will its content be changed by the facts that the various media are "increasingly geared to coverage of the ephemeral" and that "the borderline between news and entertainment is almost nonexistent; both have increasingly been centered in the personal and the scandalous" (9). Similarly, how is our doctrine reduced if its primary orientation is a political one? Johnson comments that in various ideological readings of the Scriptures,

> Jesus is pitted against the church, and the Gospels are pitted against the rest of the New Testament, but only when read against their plain sense to yield a portrait of Jesus that fits the ideological commitments of the readers.
>
> Is it any wonder that ministers shaped according to such perceptions should find themselves with little sense of how the New Testament might speak to their own situation or that of their people? Christianity is reduced to a critique of patriarchal, capitalist, homophobic society.[19] Sin is located in the structures of society, rather than

---

19. By this comment Johnson is not saying (nor am I) that patriarchal, capitalistic, and homophobic oppressions ought not to be critiqued. The problem is the reductionism, which continues to occur whenever we read the Bible politically and ideologically, instead of exegetically, theologically, and ecclesiologically.

in the hearts of people. In this understanding, talk about personal transformation, much less personal salvation, appears as counterrevolutionary. But these perceptions are scarcely those of the majority of Christians whom these ministers serve. Such Christians still expect a proclamation of the word of God that somehow is grounded in the gospel and pertains to the ultimate realities of their own lives, and not exclusively to the problems of the socially marginalized. (65-66)

Primarily Johnson is calling the Church to methods that mirror God's commitment to us. Speaking especially to seminary professors — and therefore I think to all of us concerned for building the Christian community and nurturing the Christian life — Johnson challenges us this way:

Those of us who are entrusted with the formation of Christianity's ministers and leaders ought, I think, to take less seriously the judgment of our academic colleagues and more seriously the judgment of God, "before whose judgment seat we all shall stand" (Rom. 14:10). We need to ask not only what we are teaching but also what we are failing to teach. We can begin by affirming what is positive in the gift of God in Jesus Christ and what is of astonishing and transformative power in the story of Jesus, before asking what is lacking in it and how it might need supplementing from other traditions. We should, in a word, ask of one another, before and during our criticism of the Christian tradition, an explicit and exquisite loyalty to it. (170-71)

All of us must in weakness ask about our teaching in light of the judgment of God — laying bare both our methods and the content of what we teach before God's judgment. Do we teach out of God's power or under the influence of other powers inimical to the gospel? When we criticize, do we start with a profound loyalty to the faith?

Listeners to my lectures at Pittsburgh Theological Seminary asked in the discussion periods if Johnson's comments are meant to reject all the methods of contemporary scholarship. Can any of "the world's methods" be utilized for the churches' work? Can they be adapted to our purposes without losing the gospel? Can they be transformed?

Of course, contemporary methods of scholarship offer numerous constructive gifts for our work. However, not all methods serve the Church. Because the degree of fallenness of the powers varies, we must continually learn to discern which ones are more true to their own vocation, which offer some possibility for change, and which are so incorrigible that we should refuse to collaborate with them, in order to take the side of people oppressed by those principalities. Always we must remember that the powers can be changed, not because we can make them good or cause them to be brought into subjection, but because Jesus Christ already is Lord over them.

Remember the model of Jesus' behavior, noted by Karl Barth in his 1953 lectures, as sketched in Chapter 1 of this book. Jesus did not align himself with any of the powers, nor favor any particular program. Instead he put them all in question, revealed their limits, and enjoyed the freedom of the kingdom of God.[20] Barth's comments usher me back to the necessity of recognizing our weakness, as outlined in Chapter 2, for by myself I cannot (nor can our churches corporately) reveal the limits of powers and maintain the freedom of God's kingdom. Only in death to ourselves and dependency upon the Triune God's indwelling in the community of faith can I, can we, learn to discern which powers to resist, which can be transformed, and how Christ is Lord over them and through them.

Content

Not only the methods by which doctrine is developed and decided but also its content is constantly under threat from the various powers of our society. At the 1998 Princeton Lectures on Youth, Church, and Culture, Martin Marty asked what early Christians and youth growing up in an increasingly postmodern culture have in common. The answer, he suggested, is that "who Jesus Christ as Lord was had to be determined among many altars and shrines, many banners and advertisements, many pitches and preachments, among the so-called gods and the many gods and lords."[21] In the midst of the confusing din, it is essential that we keep returning to our roots to rediscover who Jesus is as our Lord today. Catholics in recent decades

20. See this also in Rolf Joachim Erler and Reiner Marquard, eds., *A Karl Barth Reader,* trans. and ed. Geoffrey W. Bromiley (Grand Rapids: Wm. B. Eerdmans Publishing Co., 1986), p. 61.

21. Martin E. Marty, "'Who Is Jesus Christ for Us Today?' as Asked by Young People," in *Growing Up Postmodern: Imitating Christ in the Age of "Whatever,"* ed. Kenda Creasy Dean (Princeton, NJ: Institute for Youth Ministry, 1999), p. 25.

have been emphasizing this necessity of *ressourcement* or "tapping the great, replenishing sources, the ever fresh waters of a living tradition."[22]

In this broiling time of great confusions concerning the question of truth, who Jesus is remains a topic of several pointed debates. Luke Timothy Johnson elucidates

> two sets of sharply differing perceptions concerning Jesus, the Christian religion, the Church, and the New Testament. On one side is the perception of Jesus given by the Christian creed: Jesus is declared as Son of God. The significance of Jesus is not determined by his ministry alone, but above all and essentially by the mystery of his death and resurrection. For the Christian confession, the risen Lord still powerfully alive is the "real Jesus." On the other side, Jesus must be understood apart from the framework of the Christian creed: the resurrection is reduced to a series of visionary experiences of certain followers and the significance of Jesus is to be assessed entirely from the period of his ministry.
>
> Different perceptions of the Christian religion are also operative. One perspective views Christianity as based in God's self-disclosure or revelation, and therefore structured and enlivened by that self-disclosure. In this view, Christianity is regarded as a way of life rooted in and organized around a genuine experience of ultimate reality mediated by the crucified and raised Messiah, Jesus. The other perspective sees Christianity as another among the world's religions, that is, fundamentally as a cultural reality rooted in the human construction of symbolic worlds.
>
> The same difference in perspective affects understandings of the Church. One views the Church as a community answerable primarily to the sources of its own identity, whose integrity is measured by fidelity to its originating experiences and canonical writings, whose teachers and teaching are evaluated essentially in terms of their commitment to and clear expression of those resources. Another views the Church as a social organization answerable to the criteria of the society in which it finds itself; its integrity is to be measured according to the norms applied to other social and political entities, in

22. See Jean Bethke Elshtain, *Who Are We? Critical Reflections and Hopeful Possibilities* (Grand Rapids: Wm. B. Eerdmans Publishing Co., 2000), p. 4.

terms of its relevance or usefulness for the contemporary understanding and valuation of the world. (57)

I have quoted Johnson at such length because he so concisely delineates the
issues in the debate between the self-named Jesus Seminar and what is understood to be "orthodox" Christianity.

Another reduction of biblical doctrine occurs when churches sell out
to cultural powers that foster what has been called since Luther's time "a
theology of glory," as opposed to the biblical "theology of the cross." Luke
Timothy Johnson's comments about the Gnostic gospels with reference to
the Jesus Seminar also pertain to churches whose major operating mode is
success, victory, health, wealth, and other forms of power and prestige:

> Even more strikingly, the Gnostic gospels lack passion accounts. The
> death of Jesus is either omitted or touched on only lightly. . . . In the
> canonical Gospels . . . the passion accounts play a central and climac-
> tic role. The emphasis of the canonical Gospels is on the suffering of
> the Messiah. The difference in emphasis . . . has to do with percep-
> tions of how divine power works in the world. In Gnostic Christian-
> ity, the enlightenment of the mind enables the avoidance of suffering.
> In classical Christianity, the gift of the Holy Spirit leads one through
> the same path of suffering that was followed by the Messiah.
>
> I said that the canonical Gospels view Jesus from the perspective
> of the resurrection. That is true. But in sharp contrast to the Gnostic
> gospels, which have *only* that perception, the canonical Gospels hold
> that vision of power in tension with the reality of Jesus' suffering and
> death. In each of the four canonical Gospels, Jesus is portrayed in
> terms of *kenosis*, or self-emptying. In none of the canonical Gospels
> is the scandal of the cross removed in favor of the divine glory. In
> each, the path to glory passes through real suffering. Despite all the
> diversity concerning the details of Jesus' ministry, the canonical Gos-
> pels agree on this fundamental *pattern*. (150-51)

The scandal of the cross, of course, has always been a stumbling block
and an offense. Jesus asked the two disciples on the way to Emmaus, "Was
it not necessary that the Messiah should suffer these things and then enter
into his glory?" (Luke 24:26). Cleopas and his traveling companion could
hardly comprehend that God would work in such a mysterious way as

weakness. They needed Jesus' rebuke, "Oh, how foolish you are, and how slow of heart to believe all that the prophets have declared!" (v. 25) — and perhaps so do we. I wish we could all have been walking along with the three as, "beginning with Moses and all the prophets, [Jesus] interpreted to them the things about himself in all the scriptures" (v. 27).

This Jesus who fulfilled the Scriptures according to God's plan of weakness is the doctrinal content that we need in spite of various powers persuading us otherwise; this is the doctrinal content that gives us resources to withstand other powers. Johnson avers,

> The Jesus who truly challenges this age, as every age, is the one who suffers in obedience to God and calls others to such suffering service in behalf of humanity. This is the Jesus that classical Christianity has always proclaimed; this is an understanding of discipleship to which classical Christianity has always held. (177)

And this is the discipleship threatened by doctrinal bones made crooked by rejections either of our personal and corporate weakness in Christ or of God's weakness through Christ.

Our churches operate as fallen powers when the gospel is no longer a stumbling block, when the "foolishness" and "weakness" of God outlined in 1 Corinthians 1–2 are discarded in favor of status, position, wealth, popularity, acceptability to the modern or postmodern minds, or power. Only in the paradox of glory through suffering can we find the truth of God's triumph, not as an oppressive power, but in the power of submission to death. Churches have lost their vocation when they please the world too much and lose the scandal of justification by grace — the helplessness that sticks in the craw of those who want to be able to fix themselves by themselves.

The apostle Paul's saying, "For I decided to know nothing among you except Jesus Christ, and him crucified" (1 Cor. 2:2), is not very fashionable in an age that rejects the atonement as an unnecessary doctrine (though, of course, abuses of Paul's assertion — and the severe wounds caused when it is a crooked bone propped up from the outside — should be repudiated). Leon Morris's *The Cross in the New Testament* offers a thorough discussion of all the passages in the New Testament dealing with the atonement and explication of what the early Church taught on the subject. Morris's thesis is that there is substantial unity in the New Testament, though considerable variety. "It is also my conviction that there is a much more solid weight of scriptural teaching behind the view that Christ was in some sense our Substitute than most modern scholars will allow."[23]

Why is this hiddenness of God in the utter humility of Christ so ardently rejected in our times? It seems to me that much of the denunciation of the doctrine's "patriarchal oppression" derives from positions that are not fully trinitarian. Perhaps, however, the deeper reason for making this move is that we human beings really dislike having to admit the fullness of our sin and our desperate need for God to do something about it because we deserve God's punishment and wrath, and the Lamb slaughtered willingly chose to bear it for us. I know that it really galls me to acknowledge my total helplessness to be what I'd like to be, my hopelessness in the face of God's holiness, my weakness when I desire to be strong and successful. I cringe at how ridiculous is my understanding in the face of God's wisdom and Triune mysteries.

Biblically Formed Vision

For that reason we are compelled to add now a third element to our consideration of "the apostles' teaching." Not only do our methods for developing doctrine and the content of that dogma matter, but also faith's tenets are to be lived out by means of biblically formed vision and habits. If we have received the Scriptures not as a treasure to be pondered (by our training in the kingdom, Matt. 13:52), nor as a tradition of faith to be "held fast" (2 Thess. 2:15), nor as the Revelation of God,[24] but as a problem to be solved by atomizing the text, by tearing it apart, then we are no longer left with doctrine that can form our lives. The theology of weakness outlined in Chapter 2 causes Christians to see differently from how the world sees. Our goal is that we — and all the Christians our churches serve — would become biblically formed to have, as Paul says, the mind of Christ (Phil.

23. Leon Morris, *The Cross in the New Testament*, 2nd ed. (Grand Rapids: Wm. B. Eerdmans Publishing Co., 1999), p. 6.

24. Jacques Ellul taught me the importance of understanding the Revelation through "le Revélé," the Revealed One. See chapters 5 and 8, "The Contemporaneity of the Reformation" and "Innocent Notes on 'The Hermeneutic Question,'" in *Sources and Trajectories: Eight Early Articles by Jacques Ellul That Set the Stage*, trans. and ed. Marva J. Dawn (Grand Rapids: Wm. B. Eerdmans Publishing Co., 1997).

2:5-10). What would our churches be like if all the young people in them wanted more than anything to have their lives guided by the instruction of God's Word? And in a culture with a despicably "Low Information-Action Ratio,"[25] what would our churches be like if we all *acted* on what we know?

In *False Presence of the Kingdom,* Ellul critiques one form of our fallenness from doctrinal/biblical formation evidenced in our churches' and our own desire to be "up-to-the-minute" (with its correlative loss of interest in the eternal). This fallenness is manifested in the passion for the latest thing — leaving us "conformed to the world" so that "Our interest is confined to economic and social problems, *such as the world defines them, sees them and chooses to present them.*" Ellul continues,

> This last point is the heart of the matter. We put on the world's glasses in order to see only what the world sees. The Christian is characterized by the fact that he perceives problems *when* the world perceives them, and *as* it states them. He exhibits no clarity of vision which would permit him to see sooner, more deeply, or further. In my opinion, it is not a matter of intelligence, but of the Holy Spirit. . . .
>
> But if Christians thus limit themselves to a mere ratification of the world's decisions, and of its self-diagnosis; if they perceive problems when and as non-Christians claim to state them; if they associate themselves without reservation with non-Christian activities, then, of course, the way is paved for an easy contact with others. Christians, in that case, are bringing to people just what the latter expect of religion. But precisely at that moment the Christian transforms the revealed truth into a religion. He uses it to supply the wants of man and to satisfy the human heart. That, more than philosophic error, is the real transition from revelation to religion.[26]

There are many ways in which doctrinal/biblical formation is refashioned into religion (in the false sense of that word). Besides Ellul's example of thinking about everything from our society's perspectives, the other major means is when the biblical perspectives themselves are inverted.

25. See Neil Postman, *Amusing Ourselves to Death: Public Discourse in the Age of Show Business* (New York: Viking Penguin, 1985).

26. Ellul, *False Presence of the Kingdom,* pp. 48-49.

For example, the loss of the content of the atonement and of our weakness before God results in a typical reversal of law and gospel. The freedom of the Christian then becomes *our efforts* to follow Jesus' example. The consequence of the elision of Jesus' dying and rising is that we have no power to follow Jesus. We are left with our own exertions, which should have been brought to their end in the weakness of faith. I have heard too many sermons turning gospel into law.

A pastor once referred to some of my teaching, but entirely missed my point. He gave examples from the Christmas stories of spiritual exercises that we *should* follow, such as the pondering of Mary which I had described in a sermon. However, my emphasis had been not on Mary, but on how her perspective was changed when Gabriel had urged her to stop looking at herself to see *what God would do* by the overshadowing of the Holy Spirit. Her attitude, consequently, changed from "How can this be, since I am a virgin" to "Here am I, the servant of the Lord; let it be with me according to your word." What had been, in my sermon, the freedom of the gospel — God's Spirit working wonders in our weakness — was turned into the burden of law in the spiritual disciplines we should undertake. By these comments I am not negating the value of such disciplines. I simply don't want to lose the Joy of the gospel that spurs, and spills over in, our practices.

To preach law is to assert what we must do to build faith. To proclaim the gospel is to tell what God has done for us in the death and resurrection, in the continuous creation, in the sending of the Spirit. Gospel is thus sweet news for those of us who know our weakness.

A final example shows how our method might disrupt the doctrinal content and thus inhibit a life of biblically formed faith. Consider the story of the healing of the lepers — how do we view that narrative? We know we are seeing ourselves as too strong if we identify first with Jesus as the healer and not with the lepers who desperately need to be healed.

2. Fellowship

One thing we will discover as we work through the seven practices of the early Church is how intertwined they are. After doctrine, Acts 2 lists fellowship, but this doesn't mean the casual sort of interaction we might have in a "fellowship hour" after a worship service. As we saw in Luke Timothy

Johnson's comments above, media handling of doctrinal issues is a fellowship issue. The Church as a study/discussion community has been violated. The community is even more fractured by political maneuverings.

Fellowship in the early Christian Church meant serious commitment, following the one who said that he lay down his life for his friends. Genuine community, then, means being continually, strenuously devoted to one another in the congregation. Since the root meaning of the Greek word for "fellowship" is "having in common," it means sharing deeply in each other's needs and carrying one another's burdens.

True weakness — that is, a genuine fulfillment of the Church's true vocation as a power — is found, for example, in vulnerability to our brothers' and sisters' needs (Rom. 12), openness to each other's rebukes (1 Thess. 5:12, 14), genuine hospitality to the needy (Matt. 25) and to other saints (2 and 3 John). This fellowship is violated by such powers as business policies,[27] mammon, technology, and even democracy, when these are stretched beyond their proper vocation.

My own behavior while giving the Schaff Lectures is a good example (that is, a bad example!) of the destruction of fellowship. Present business policies teach us to be efficient,[28] and my desire to get as much done as possible in preparation for the next day's lecture made me unwilling one evening to linger in conversation with a person who was questioning the powers at work among the poor. When I apologized to him the next day, I discovered that the loss was entirely mine, for he had deep experiences that would have given me many insights.

Technology, similarly, can disrupt true fellowship. I know some church staffs who never talk with each other face to face, but simply send e-mails throughout the offices. The gifts and benefits of e-mail are enormous, but for this very reason the use of this technology is hardly ever questioned. As Australian commentator Hugh Mackay remarks,

27. Charles M. Olsen's *Transforming Church Boards into Communities of Spiritual Leaders* (Bethesda, MD: Alban Institute, 1995) is extremely helpful for equipping the leaders of churches to serve out of spiritual, rather than business, policies.

28. Jacques Ellul shows profoundly in his technology trilogy how *the* major criterion of our technological world is efficiency. See (preferably in this order) Jacques Ellul, *The Technological Society,* trans. John Wilkinson (New York: Vintage Books, 1964); *The Technological System,* trans. Joachim Neugroschel (New York: The Continuum Publishing Company, 1980); and *The Technological Bluff,* trans. Joyce Main Hanks (Grand Rapids: Wm. B. Eerdmans Publishing Co., 1990).

Everything from the printed staff newspaper to e-mail has its proper place in the total information system of an organisation, but whenever we fall for the trap of thinking that the dispensing of information *is* communication, we are in serious trouble. Communication rarely occurs in the absence of face-to-face contact.[29]

I urge every pastor to ask himself or herself, "Does e-mail actually help my ministry more than it distracts from it?" We will all answer that question differently according to the type of work we do primarily — and for many e-mail is a great boon — but many professional leaders have responded to this question by recognizing that they waste more time on extraneous mail than they gain with the technology's efficiency.

One pastor called to tell me that he'd "given up e-mail for good!" When I asked, "Why?" he reported that he had discovered that it made his relationships more shallow, that it did not promote his creativity or keep him accountable, that he couldn't tell the tone of the person with whom he was "conversing," that he found himself responding really fast and more harshly — and, whereas a letter might have been retrieved and torn up, there was no way to call back an e-mail that had already been sent.

His resolve to give up e-mail completely might be unique, but his points are worth pondering. Neil Postman suggested in a lecture at a 1997 conference on technology and education at Penn State that we should ask of every new system or technique, "What problem do I have that this technology solves?" To that I would append, "without adding so many complications that the benefits are outweighed by the disadvantages." Our major goal, we have to keep remembering, is not simply to use technology or to be efficient, but to deepen the genuine fellowship of, and communication in, our churches.

On the congregational/corporate level, churches often overlook the concerns of individuals in the attempt to be efficient. "Majority vote" is one of the best gifts of democracy, but the process destroys genuine fellowship in the community of faith when it is allowed to turn us into "winners" and "losers" on issues. Rather, the early Church continued to discuss matters until all the people could say "it has seemed good to the Holy Spirit and to us" (Acts 15:28). I have experienced in a Mennonite congregation this wonderful gift of consensus and corporate discernment

29. Mackay, *Turning Point,* p. 102.

and wish churches would never make decisions based on majority vote again. Consensus takes more time (it is definitely not efficient to hear everyone's concerns), but in the long run, it seems to me, a parish would know more deeply and with more unity the direction of God's guiding Spirit.

On the other hand, true fellowship is marred if a congregation tries to bear *all* the world's suffering, if we try to extend our community concern beyond our own vocation. As Jacques Ellul comments,

> It is enough to bear [the suffering] of one's neighbor. Once again, we encounter the very bad presumption of putting ourselves in the place of Jesus Christ. . . .
>
> That does not mean that we are to be indifferent to the sufferings of mankind! But it does mean that my only actual concern is the one which is near enough to me, and close enough to my size, so that I might *really* do something about it. Revelation, in its rigorous realism, does not ask us to torture ourselves over universal ideas and information, nor to lose sleep over news items from everywhere. As Paul says so well: "For if the readiness is there, it is acceptable according to what a man has, not according to what he has not" (2 Corinthians 8:12).[30]

Certainly we need the discernment of the entire community for a church to hear the Spirit's directions for the limits of our capacities to care.

Mammon is another power that certainly fractures fellowship. Right now I know of congregations being split over tactics for raising money, over decisions about how to spend it, over questions concerning whether to remain in poor neighborhoods or to move to more "attractive" environs, over whether to create and finance new staff positions or to use that money for building projects or program expenditures. We will look more closely at other dimensions of church economics later in this chapter and in the next. Similarly, issues of homogeneity and dimensions of worship as destructive of true fellowship will be addressed in other sections.

---

30. Ellul, *False Presence of the Kingdom*, pp. 70-71.

3. The Breaking of THE Bread

The "breaking of *the* bread" (as the Greek of Acts 2:42 literally reads, as opposed to "breaking bread" in verse 46) is the New Testament idiom for the celebration of the eucharist or Lord's Supper. This tradition of the early Christian community is often violated in our times and is, like most of the practices, closely connected to the fellowship of the Church. The apostle Paul insists in 1 Corinthians 11 that gathering together for the breaking of the bread involves "discerning the Body of Christ," which meant, especially for the people of Corinth where the rich were taking advantage of poorer members, to recognize Christ in *all* the members of the Body and in the members *together*. Consequently, whenever we "break the bread" we are called to care for the poor, to eliminate class distinctions between the people of our world. We remember the sufferings of Jesus and therefore care about the sufferings of our neighbors.

But this practice takes us beyond hospitality concerns to understanding Jesus' Supper as sacrament and then understanding our role in the world as sacramental. Jean-Pierre de Caussade, a Jesuit priest who lived in the late 1600s and first half of the 1700s, taught that to be sacramental is to be totally surrendered to God so that God lives through us by grace.[31] When churches do not live in such weakness, they serve not as icons (or windows through which the world sees God), but as graphics for themselves.

To live "the breaking of the bread" with congregational integrity — without any barriers between peoples, without any segregations based on economics, race, or musical style — demands great weakness. Many of the church marketing gurus advocate churches of homogeneity, appealing to those who are like us so that our churches will grow, but this violates the sacrament of Christ's presence and destroys our testimony to the world that there are no divisions and distinctions among the people of God.

Instead, in the early Church the eucharist as

the common meal signified the oneness of the community under the sovereign Lordship of Christ — an allegiance subversive with respect to imperial rule — and made visible in the sharing of their common

31. Jean-Pierre de Caussade, *The Sacrament of the Present Moment,* trans. Kitty Muggeridge (San Francisco: Harper & Row, Publishers, 1982).

life, with an implicit economic dimension (Acts 2:44-45; 4:32-35; 1 Cor 11:20-34). It quite simply proclaimed and revealed the reality of a new creation, a new social world.[32]

For there to be a new creation, the old self must know its weakness and die to its own prejudices, tastes, class structures, and personal desires. How can we share this eschatological feast if we don't participate in displaying God's future, in which all will be equally fed and we will all join together in universal praise? It seems to me that if we eat the body and blood of Christ in expensive churches without care for the hungry, the sacrament is no longer a foretaste of the feast to come, but a trivialized picnic to which not everyone is invited.

There are many practical questions about celebrating the Lord's Supper that each congregation must thoroughly discuss occasionally — to be sure that we keep remembering why we do this. Amidst the arguments about intinction versus common or individual cups, about the kind of bread to use, and so forth, probably the most important controversy centers on the frequency of celebration. In light of the themes of this book, it seems to me that churches would favor frequent celebration in this three-fold fulfillment of the Church's true vocation as a power:

> to recognize our weakness and our need for a Savior and, consequently, to desire to commemorate, as Jesus commanded us, his past sufferings on our behalf;
> to strengthen us to live with Christ's power tabernacling in us by being an icon of his suffering presence for the sake of the world at the present time;
> to look forward to the future, as Jesus promised, when we will eat this feast in his glorious presence and celebrate forever the culmination of his cosmic reconciliation.

The last is an especially important reminder lest we fall into the common temptation of thinking that by our power we bring in the kingdom. The mystery of Christ's passion and glorification is that we participate in it, but not to bring it about. Our hope is a present reality, but our weakness prevents us from "realizing" it. If our churches overstep their true voca-

---

32. Kellermann, *Seasons of Faith and Conscience*, p. 115.

tion, then they cannot serve as a sacrament in the world, as a visible reality incarnating the invisible kingdom. As Jacques Ellul insisted, we are citizens of two cities and we do belong to both, but we must not make the error of believing that by constant progress in the human order we shall attain the kingdom of God or that we can produce the kingdom.[33] Instead,

It is a matter of mingling with the world while strictly refusing to be lost, while retaining the specific character, the uniqueness of the truth revealed in Jesus Christ and of the new life we have received from him. It is a matter of supplying the savor of the salvation, of the truth, of the freedom and of the love which are in Christ, and never letting oneself be taken over by the perdition of the world, with its strength, its splendor, and its efficiency![34]

Celebration of the eucharist supplies the savor, declares God's truth, and reminds us that we serve out of weakness and not out of the world's strength. This meal, which makes no sense to those outside the Church, enables us both to display and to wait for God's own future. Both sides of that eschatological dialectic (the "already, but not yet" of the Church's life) are destroyed by the contemporary techniques of "church growth," which suggest that churches eliminate the Supper because it doesn't "appeal" to outsiders. We easily forget that, as John Zizioulas asserts, it is the eucharist that constitutes the Church (and not the reverse),[35] for in this meal the absence of Jesus becomes a presence.[36]

33. Ellul, *Presence of the Kingdom*, pp. 44-48. See also a proper interpretation of Martin Luther's doctrine of the two kingdoms (a doctrine frequently misunderstood and misapplied) in Heinrich Bornkamm, *Luther's Doctrine of the Two Kingdoms: In the Context of His Theology*, trans. Karl H. Hertz (Philadelphia: Fortress Press, 1966).

34. Ellul, *False Presence of the Kingdom*, p. 43.

35. John D. Zizioulas, *Being as Communion: Studies in Personhood and the Church* (Crestwood, NY: St. Vladimir's Press, 1985), pp. 20ff.

36. See Douglas Farrow, *Ascension and Ecclesia: On the Significance of the Doctrine of the Ascension for Ecclesiology and Christian Cosmology* (Grand Rapids: Wm. B. Eerdmans Publishing Co., 2000), for a thorough discussion of the importance of this mystery.

4. Prayers

This fourth practice of the early Church involves spending time in earnest prayer for one another and for the needs of the larger community and the world, in practicing the presence of God so that we might know the Triune mind for our lives and service. The fullness of the prayer life of the early Church is hinted at in the Pauline corpus, which contains numerous comments about praying without ceasing, asking the saints to "pray also for me," thanking God for them "every time I remember you," and reminding them to pray for their leaders and the civil authorities.

Of course, prayer is a topic (as all of these are) much too large to discuss thoroughly here, so let me simply sketch two ways in which churches act as fallen powers with respect to prayer. The first is that we often approach wrongly the social problems surrounding our congregations because of a paucity of prayer. Instead of allowing our minds to be transformed by the presence and truth of God through prayer, we fall into what Jacques Ellul calls "the political illusion"[37] caused by the media, which includes these effects:

> the inability to grasp a political or economic situation as a whole, a weakness of political thought, an ignorance of the various levels on which political action takes place, and a blindness to the fact that the most recent and spectacular is always the least important and the least decisive.[38]

Again, Ellul's overstatement that "the most recent and spectacular is *always* the least important and . . . decisive" must be qualified. However, we must also ask why it is that churches so easily jump on trendy bandwagons, fall for the most up-to-date fads, look for the most "exciting" approaches to issues, and make radical changes without adequate prayer and searching for the mind of Christ.[39]

What Ellul primarily objects to is that churches with inadequate prayer

37. See Jacques Ellul, *The Political Illusion*, trans. Konrad Kellen (New York: Alfred A. Knopf, 1967).

38. Ellul, *False Presence of the Kingdom*, p. 93. Page references to this book in the following paragraphs will be given parenthetically in the text.

39. For examples, see Philip D. Kenneson and James L. Street, *Selling Out the Church: The Dangers of Church Marketing* (Nashville: Abingdon Press, 1997).

come to social problems with the culture's perspective, instead of our uniquely Christian one. In George Lindbeck's phrasing, we should instead let the biblical text be that "which absorbs the world, rather than the world the text."[40] Remember Jacques Ellul's complaint, recorded above, asking that Christians be guided by the Holy Spirit to "see sooner, more deeply, or further."

Part of the "more deeply" that Ellul longs for Christians to see is the reality of the principalities and powers and their effect upon the world and upon our churches. His reference to the Holy Spirit reminds us that these spiritual matters, including the nature and work of the demonic spirits, can be discerned only in spiritual ways, only by prayer. How essential it is in these days for the Church's task of prayerful discernment to be restored!

Without it churches resort to politics (both internal and external), without Christian perspective. Ellul is not advocating political withdrawal or provincialism; rather, he urges us to know more clearly how Christians should be involved in political matters. He suggests that a twofold judgment and meaning has been revealed by Scripture. Thus,

> it is precisely the demonic character of the power which makes prayer the most important political action that the Christian could possibly take, prayer which is a sharing in the struggle of Jesus Christ, prayer that the authorities might be brought into subjection, prayer that they might be exorcised, prayer that their power might be turned toward justice and good. Prayer is much more important than all the declarations, demonstrations, elections, etc. . . .
>
> If the Christian is to do more than respect and obey, he must in any case realize that he is entering the most dangerous territory, a demonic domain; for if the authorities have been conquered by Jesus Christ, they nevertheless retain, throughout the duration of our history, their demonic capabilities, their power to rebel against the Lord, their tendency toward evil through disobedience to the order assigned them by God. (112-13)

Thus, the Church must realize that often, when she has become involved in politics, the result has been "her own betrayal and an abandonment of the truth of the Gospel" (118). Ellul insists,

40. See Lindbeck, *The Nature of Doctrine*, p. 118.

When all is said and done, it seems as though politics is the Church's worst problem. It is her constant temptation, the occasion of her greatest disasters, the trap continually set for her by the Prince of this world.

The proposal is made to the Church on every occasion to give expression to her faith in the political order, to act effectively, for once, on the course of this world through the avenue of politics. She is forever being reminded that she cannot remain a stranger to the actual life of people. And she walks, each time, precisely into the blind alley of abandoning what is specifically hers, her unique vocation. Each time she is transformed into a power in bondage to the world.

Yet we must continually remind ourselves that the opposite attitude has not more truth on its side. The review of successive historical betrayals by the Church through political involvement does not signify that the Church ought to be spiritual, that the faith is a matter of the personal and the inward, that revelation is purely abstract, that the contest for truth has no political implications and that the love imperative has no social significance. All that spirituality is just as false, treasonous and hypocritical as the taking of political sides condemned above. It is a negation of the incarnation, a forgetting of the lordship of Jesus Christ. It is to scorn one's neighbor (whose life is affected by the political, the economic and the social). It implies that we acquiesce in giving a free hand to the Prince of this world. It is the rejection of everything Jesus tells us about the Kingdom of Heaven. It is the *other trap* which Satan lays in the path of the Church. (126)

When Ellul wrote the original French version of *False Presence of the Kingdom* in 1963, he didn't elaborate that second trap because he thought the first, the wrong-headed political involvement, was the primary threat to the Church's mission in his day (127). It seems to me that in our day both politics contrary to the Church's vocation and also spirituality abstracted from the issues of the world are significant threats! Only by diligent prayer can our churches avoid either betrayal of their proper mission.

The second primary way in which churches demonstrate fallenness with respect to prayer concerns internal politics and the motives from which public prayer is offered. Sometimes leaders use it to manipulate people. Once at the congregational meeting of a divided parish, I observed a pastor who prayed for unity, but made it clear by the vocabulary and structure of his prayer that such unity had to be bought according to his terms. The people felt clobbered by his prayer, not brought into the presence of God. Every time we pray with an agenda, we exert power falsely and violate our vocation as the praying Church.

5. Signs and Wonders

In an age of unimaginable technological contraptions and mind-boggling visual effects, of virtual reality and phenomenal paraphernalia, do we even think about the biblical signs and wonders? Have our churches given up talking about them?

In the early Church *fear* came upon every soul because of the signs and wonders being done by the apostles, but are our present-day spiritual leaders acting similarly as agents of miraculous healings? Or have we so much let the power of technology become an idolatry that we no longer even recognize GOD's power at work in every medical wonder? Do our churches notice the signs of God's mysterious interventions? Do we observe and praise the power of God at work through us?

Medical wonders are difficult to speak about in a society that has given up care for cure. Our brilliant technology keeps doctors heavily involved in a patient's case as long as there is hope that some technique will prolong life, yet as soon as there appears to be no other resource the care seems to evaporate.[41] Yet you probably know people, as do I, who have made miraculous recoveries or have come to an entirely new sense of peace in their final hours. Just last week my elderly neighbor — to everyone's surprise — came away from the brink of death (though she was certainly ready for it) to wonder at God's mysterious purposes for her continued life.

Churches move away from the healing signs of the early Church in two ways. On the one hand, most (predominately mainline?) churches don't seem to believe in their ministry to heal (though even secular studies are discovering that prayer has an effect on healing). Many years ago I was roused from my own doubts about such a ministry by Roy Lawrence's *Christian Healing Rediscovered*, which investigates the New Testament

41. See Richard Lischer, "Living by the Word: A Sense of Ending," *Christian Century* 116, no. 8 (10 March 1999): 277.

commands of Jesus to his disciples to "enter a town . . . ; cure the sick who are there, and say to them, 'The kingdom of God has come near to you'" (Luke 10:8-9).[42] Why have we forgotten that when Jesus called his disciples together he "gave them power and authority over all demons and to cure diseases, and he sent them out to proclaim the kingdom of God and to heal" (Luke 9:1-2)?

I excused myself — I don't have the gift of healing, I thought — but really I was doubting what God can do. The next week I was visiting friends, and the husband complained that he had been ill for several weeks with a mysterious malady for which the doctors knew no solution. Haunted by Roy Lawrence's gentle admonishment, I told my friend that I felt burdened to pray for his healing and proceeded to lay my hands on his head and to verbalize a very faltering prayer. To my utter amazement, he was better the next day. Why was I so surprised?

Such an incident has never happened again, so I'm not claiming any special gift with this illustration. I intend simply to raise the question: Why do our churches not engage in ministries of healing? (I'm grateful, I must add, that many more congregations now are offering services of prayer and healing and that many clergy conferences are including such services.)

Perhaps we don't emphasize healing because the whole idea has been so abused in Christian history. Many "healing" ministries are fake, manipulative, oppressive, greedy. Some churches (predominately evangelical?) fall to the opposite extreme of making this ministry too prominent an aspect in their mission or making people feel guilty if they don't experience physical healing. Both problems turn the church into a fallen power.

When we make healing too prominent a focus, we mistake the meaning of the biblical signs. In the Schaff Lectures I gave this illustration: If I see a sign pointing to Pittsburgh Theological Seminary, I certainly wouldn't park my car at the sign and hang around there. But the sign is a real and true thing, offering the gift of its pointing to the greater reality, the actual seminary and its people and scholarship. The Gospel writer John uses the word *signs* (rather than the *miracles* of the Synoptics) to emphasize that they point to the reality of Christ and are recorded so that we might believe who Jesus is (John 20:30-31). Do our churches function as signs to the greater reality of Christ, or do we want people to "park their car" in the

---

42. Roy Lawrence, *Christian Healing Rediscovered* (Downers Grove, IL: InterVarsity Press, 1980).

idolatry of a certain kind of physical healing or a certain church? My neighbor's reaction to her surprising extension of life illustrates an excellent response to the sign of her healing; she knew that it pointed to God and readied herself for what she might learn about/from God with this gift.

Signs are also misunderstood if we demand a particular kind of healing. We hear people "claim" in prayer a specific physical miracle — which is certainly to overstep our proper vocation as pray-ers. God has many ways to heal. How can we exercise our true weakness and simply rest our requests within Triune grace? How can we learn to see and not block out all the emotional, intellectual, social, physical, and spiritual healings that God is constantly providing? And how can we learn as churches that all the members and the whole Body together have a vocation to bring healing to others?

Let us turn to an entirely different kind of "wonder" and consider God's interventions in the world. Here our churches err because we don't look for such interventions and don't praise God for them, nor do we display them to the world, but look instead to the powers of society to remedy situations. What Jacques Ellul says about political options could also be said about all the dimensions of our lives (such as the medical or social or financial):

> Now the Church should be there precisely to affirm that there is another way, that there is an option, unseen by man but infinitely real, that there is a dimension to the affair which is unknown to man, that there is a truth above and beyond the political alternatives which has its repercussions on them.[43]

As perhaps the most prominent example, we can think of the immensely surprising fall of the Berlin Wall in 1989 and the breakup of the U.S.S.R. thereafter. The whole world was astonished by this dramatic turn of events (as also by the election of Nelson Mandela in South Africa or the successful overthrow of Marcos in the Philippines). Did we Christians believe that God could accomplish such an intervention? As Jörg Swoboda recounts in *The Revolution of the Candles: Christians in the Revolution of the German Democratic Republic*, "God had another plan! 'God rules,' Karl

---

43. Ellul, *False Presence of the Kingdom*, p. 163.

Barth once said to his friend Eduard Thurneysen. God intercedes and dictators go, walls cave in, people awaken, and nations break out of their bondage. And where was our faith?"[44]

We rarely expect or notice such wonders because we trust our own power to accomplish things, our own inventiveness to create things, our own wisdom to solve things, our own technology to master things. How often do we notice God at work in human skills, ingenuity, insight; in God's creation of human bodies, imaginations, memories; in God's amazing grace as it is manifested in the startling twists of history?

One other dimension of the churches' loss of signs and wonders that must be mentioned is our loss of confidence in the preaching of the Word (the second vocation besides healing for which Jesus sent out the disciples). In some places these days it is hard to find churches and pastors who focus on "rightly explaining the word of truth" (2 Tim. 2:15) when our world is more interested in its own spectacles.

It seems that more and more preachers are veering toward the kind of popular oratory fashionable in Corinth at the time that Paul wrote to that city. Then, as Timothy Savage discovered, "Since people wanted to be amused, preachers specialised in startling effects, sensational topics and powerful deliveries."[45] Just as today, in those days, "With so much emphasis on show, there was little interest in doctrine," and a high value was placed on toleration (31). Even as pluralism prevailed then as now, "The person who advocated one religion to the exclusion of the others brought ridicule and abuse upon himself" (32).

Because of all our technological wonders, are we failing to live out of the weakness that displays God's power? Do we rely on "exciting" video clips and power point presentations or on the truthful power of God's Word? Please know that I don't deny the usefulness of video or computer technology, but we must ask if we depend on Technique to convince people of the truth of the gospel rather than on the One who is the Truth. How

---

44. Jörg Swoboda, *The Revolution of the Candles: Christians in the Revolution of the German Democratic Republic*, ed. Richard V. Pierard, trans. Edwin P. Arnold (Macon, GA: Mercer University Press, 1996), p. 129.

45. Timothy B. Savage, *Power Through Weakness: Paul's Understanding of the Christian Ministry in 2 Corinthians*, Society for New Testament Studies Monograph Series 86 (Cambridge: Cambridge University Press, 1996), p. 30. Page references to this book in the rest of this paragraph will be given parenthetically in the text.

do we best bring spiritual judgments to bear on people's lives? How do our churches best speak the prophetic Word?

Why is it that so many people can talk freely about how great their church is, but find it much more difficult to converse with others about the greatness of their Lord? "Charismatic" pastors, "thrilling" worship leaders, "dynamic" musicians, or "exciting" worship services frequently become what is worshiped instead. Then we, the spiritual leaders, get so easily addicted to praise and flattery — which makes us desperate for a regular "fix" of flattery. In the classical world, the opposite of "friend" was "flatterer."[46] It takes great courage to resist these idolatrous powers, to not require adulation, but rather to be accountable to friends who love us enough to rebuke us, to be faithful to the Word and to a theology of weakness and the cross.

A young pastor from a small church in Canada that is experiencing revival and renewed discipleship said to me during a conference break, "I don't know how it started or why it started, but we are just trying to be faithful." Is this not a wonder?

Is revival not happening in our churches because we haven't become open enough to see God's signs and wonders, weak enough for God to move in with power?

6. Economic Redistribution

One of the most thrilling practices of the early Christians was their owning possessions in common so that they could have more resources to share with those in need. Could we, similarly, live more simply and more generously?

The Bible is filled with instructions to care for those whose lives are filled with sorrows — especially the poor, the homeless, the widow and orphan, the sojourner. The First Testament Jubilee, in particular, calls for restoration of the land, sustenance for those who falter, employment for those in debt (Lev. 25). Jesus, who had nowhere to lay his head, invites disciples to imitate him (Matt. 8:20) and to sell all and give it to the poor (Matt. 19:21). If so much of the Bible deals with wealth and the problems of

---

46. I learned this from Martha Ellen Stortz's *PastorPower* (Nashville: Abingdon Press, 1993), p. 116.

mammon and with such strong invitations to give, then why are our churches so rich? Why are we? Why have we made mammon such a god in our personal and corporate lives?

Dorothy Day said to Robert Coles, "I have always thought that a certain kind of success could be a sign of our ruin. We are meant to be with the poor . . . and the distractions of the mighty should be a warning to us: that we not be blinded by their glitter."[47]

The wealth of our communities is not a new problem. God's people in the First Testament also amassed wealth while others in their limited world were impoverished by their greediness. As Mark Vander Vennen describes it,

> To begin, a word came to Israel, says Isaiah (v. 8): a light in the darkness, a bar of oppression broken, a Prince of Peace coming, justice and righteousness established, a Jubilee economic rhythm of care vindicated (Isa 9:1-7).
>
> [But Israel chose another way.] . . . Faced with the light, the Israelites chose the route of the other nations and redoubled their efforts at self-aggrandizement and ambition. . . . The Israelites could build [their] stone mansions . . . only if they trampled on the poor and took from them levies of grain (Amos 5:11).[48]

Economics is perhaps the dimension in which Western Christianity is most often subverted by the powers. Jacques Ellul was a prophet who recognized the immense danger that mammon poses for churches in our times. In his chapter on the chief forms of the subversion of Christianity, he immediately lists Christendom's alliance with the powers, which arose out of the conviction that the powers had been vanquished and, therefore, could be put into the service of the gospel. What actually happens, however, is the exact opposite, for churches become penetrated by power and, consequently, are turned away from the truth by that corruption.[49] Moreover, theologians and church leaders have tried to justify and legitimize the

---

47. Coles, *Dorothy Day,* p. 134.

48. Brian Walsh, Richard Middleton, Mark Vander Vennen, and Sylvia Keesmaat, *The Advent of Justice: A Book of Meditations* (Sioux City, IA: Dordt College Press, 1993), p. 45.

49. Ellul, *The Subversion of Christianity,* pp. 20-21.

powers by showing that there is no contradiction, especially between wealth and Jesus Christ.[50]

Perhaps we need to be confronted with the glaring blatancy of the contradiction. Consider the situation in our world: in 1999 Bill Gates, Paul Allen, and Steve Balmar of Microsoft had almost $140 billion in assets — more than the combined gross national product of 43 least-developed countries and their 600 million people. Or a trivia question that is hardly trivial: On what item did U.S. citizens spend more than the gross national product of 90 nations (out of the world's 130)? The answer: trash bags!

Craig Blomberg cites depressing statistics about the amounts of money spent by Americans on soft drinks and legalized gambling, among other luxuries, compared with the amounts given to charitable organizations by Americans and, particularly, by Christians.[51] Yet, Blomberg laments, "Money, at worst, is seen as a neutral entity, and structural evil is seldom discussed." Then, in a footnote, Blomberg refers to books by Ellul[52] and Foster[53] as "important studies of the potentially diabolical seduction of material possessions," grieving that "these works have not commanded nearly the following that they deserve."[54]

Will my call also fall on deaf ears? The fact that so many of our churches rely so much on money demonstrates our inability to be weak so that we can see God's tabernacling power. Christians in the Two-Thirds World see miracles of provision ("signs and wonders"!) that we North Americans will never see as long as we rely on our own stewardship gimmicks and charitable tax deductions.

Could suburban churches partner with inner city churches to share financial and other resources? If they do, will the rich churches know their weakness enough to receive the immense gifts of their poorer brothers and sisters? Can the First World churches invite their members to desacralize

50. Ellul, *The Subversion of Christianity*, p. 33.

51. Craig L. Blomberg, *Neither Poverty nor Riches: A Biblical Theology of Material Possessions*, New Studies in Biblical Theology, series editor D. A. Carson (Grand Rapids: Wm. B. Eerdmans Publishing Co., 1999), pp. 19-20.

52. See Jacques Ellul, *Money and Power*, trans. LaVonne Neff (Downers Grove, IL: InterVarsity Press, 1984).

53. See Richard J. Foster, *The Challenge of the Disciplined Life: Christian Reflection on Money, Sex and Power* (San Francisco: Harper and Row, 1989).

54. Blomberg, *Neither Poverty nor Riches*, p. 26.

money in their own lives to work for global economic redistribution? Can we issue prophetic challenges to our members involved in multinational corporations to cease practices that exploit citizens of poorer nations? How might our church budgets be radically realigned for the sake of exposing mammon, disarming it, and triumphing over it in our corporate congregational life and in the personal lives of members?

In *Money and Power* Jacques Ellul is especially insightful because he recognizes that mammon can become a god whether we are too rich (and hoard our wealth), or too poor (and consequently covet it), or even if we have just the right amount (and never live sacrificially or generously because we are "such good stewards"). All the powers have subtle forms that deceive us into thinking that we are safely beyond their temptations or that they don't overstep their vocations. That is why this chapter is intended to stir constant questions, lest we succumb to powers which suggest that we can be Church on our own, or that any success models (numbers, money, etc.) are reliable measures of our faithfulness.

I was goaded recently to recognize afresh how — if our thinking is not undergirded with deep prayer, profound contemplation, and serious cultural analysis — we can easily go in wrong directions with economic concerns. *Atlantic Monthly* published several articles highlighting the arrogance of wealthy nations who insist that poorer countries adhere to tighter standards for reducing pollution or greenhouse gases that contribute to global warming. Daniel Sarewitz (research scholar at Columbia University's Center for Science, Policy and Outcomes) and Roger Pielke Jr. (scientist with the Environmental and Societal Impacts Group at the National Center for Atmospheric Research) argue in "Breaking the Global-Warming Gridlock" that "The implicit moral imperative is not to prevent human disruption of the environment but to ameliorate the social and political conditions that lead people to behave in environmentally disruptive ways." They quote the *China Daily,* which reported during the 1997 Kyoto "Conference of the Parties" (181 world nations ratifying an international treaty of March 1994):

> The United States . . . and other nations made the irresponsible demand . . . that the developing countries should make commitments to limiting greenhouse gas emissions. . . . As a developing country, China has 60 million poverty-stricken people and China's per capita gas emissions are only one-seventh of the average amount of more

developed countries. Ending poverty and developing the economy must still top the agenda of [the] Chinese government.[55]

Similarly, William Langewiesche critiques environmentalists, particularly Greenpeace, for their moral arrogance in denouncing the "shipbreakers" who work particularly in India, Pakistan, and Bangladesh to dismantle approximately 700 huge commercial shipping vessels annually. Langewiesche reports,

> Nagarsheth [one of the leaders in the industry] seemed to worry that I would understand the country in some antiseptic way — for its computer industry, its novelists, or maybe even its military might. But the India he wanted me to see was a place that related directly to Alang [the major shipbreaking city] — an India drowning in the poverty of its people. And so, rather than talking any more about shipbreaking, he insisted on showing me around Bombay. He guided me into the city's slums, which are said to be the largest in the world. Then he led me back toward the city center, for miles through a roadside hell where peasants lived wall-to-wall in scrap boxes and shacks, and naked children sat listless in the traffic's blue smoke as if waiting to die. Nagarsheth said, "Do you see this? Do you see this? You need to remember it when you get to Alang."[56]

Later one of the nephews of a manager of a shipbreaking operation asked him "nastily, 'The question I want to ask the environmentalists is if you should want to die first of starvation or pollution.'" When Langewiesche responded, "They say you don't have to make that choice," the nephew's simple response was, "That's bullshit." Langewiesche concludes, "In a place like Alang, he was probably right" (46). His lead-in to his article summarizes this conclusion from his intensive study:

> At Alang, in India, on a six-mile stretch of oily, smoky beach, 40,000 men work to tear apart half of the world's discarded ships, each one a

---

55. Daniel Sarewitz and Roger Pielke Jr., "Breaking the Global-Warming Gridlock," *Atlantic Monthly* 286, no. 1 (July 2000): 62.

56. William Langewiesche, "The Shipbreakers," *Atlantic Monthly* 286, no. 2 (August 2000): 43. Page references to this article in the following paragraph will be given parenthetically in the text.

sump of toxic waste. Environmentalists in the West are outraged. The shipbreakers, of course, want to be left alone — and maybe they should be. (31)

Isn't it our responsibility as followers of Jesus, as Church, to channel God's gifts differently to make it more likely that the choice between death by starvation or by pollution does not have to be made?

Jean Bethke Elshtain asserts, "The first question Christian theologians should ask is, Given God's economy toward us, how does our inevitable participation in the material goods of this world reflect that economy?"[57] For example, what would happen if we applied God's economy and God's concern for the poor to decisions about weddings in our churches?

I won't even hazard a guess at how much is spent for the average church wedding (when $10,000 for one bridal gown is not out of the ordinary), but can the fortunes expended be compatible with true fellowship, with God's commands, when people are starving? One nearby pastor suggests to each bridal couple that they give to the church (for its mission) a tithe of what they spend on their wedding — a great suggestion, I think.

In addition, could we be more strong in urging betrothed couples to reconsider seriously what a wedding means and how it should be conducted and what really matters? How do we keep God at the center and offer a wedding ceremony that is genuine worship?

My husband and I keep realizing that the best memories of our "alternative" wedding relate to the participation of friends and family — who helped me pick out the material and found the seamstress to make my dress, crocheted a slipper for my casted foot, decorated my crutches with roses and ribbons, read the Scriptures, brought foods for or served at the potluck reception, typed and duplicated the wedding folders, offered music in the worship service, and so forth. It was pure bliss to us — no frenzies, lots of fellowship in music practices and meals together, the great Joy of worship! And our request to bring an offering for the poor instead of gifts (we were both middle-aged, after all, and well established in household goods) generated a large sum for the local homeless shelter.

When our whole culture is organized around success, defined usually by the "bottom line" of money; when leaders search for outcomes that boost their own egos; when marketing bases its entire analysis of results on vari-

57. Elshtain, *Who Are We?* p. 54.

ous numbers — when these traits are nigh unto universal, how can pastors survive this onslaught, this assault? How do we immunize churches against such measurements? How do we create the kind of character that is necessary to avoid these temptations of the powers? Ministry — and being Church — tests every part of one's character. Economic redistribution is one way to counteract these forces.

7. Worship

The early Christians enjoyed meeting regularly in the temple for worship as well as in each other's homes to share meals with gladness. How has it happened that churches now frequently turn worship into a means for "sheep stealing" and competition with other churches for numbers? If in genuine worship we defeat other principalities and powers by acknowledging the only true God, why is it that our conversations about, and practices for, worship are filled with so many idolatries?

We have to remember that Jesus was opposed not to the worship in the Temple, but to its abuses. He shed tears of love for Jerusalem and longed for it to praise God and serve human life. How much he must grieve over the religious attitudes of today, which closely parallel what Timothy Savage discovered about those of the Corinthians at the time Paul wrote his letters to them:

> [T]he Corinthians . . . placed a *higher* premium on social prominence and self-display, on personal power and boasting. Likewise, they were *more* inclined to honour success and reward primacy and *more* prone to ridicule the poor and humble. When Corinthians evaluated each other they looked for the same symbols of worth which they prized for themselves — wealth, assertive speech, abusive behaviour, a head carried high, anything which might elevate them above their neighbours.
>
> The same values influenced their perspective of religion. It mattered little who the gods were or what the cults taught. What was important was whether one's needs were being met.[58]

58. Savage, *Power Through Weakness*, p. 52.

I have already discussed extensively in my two books on worship various ways in which churches fall to other powers (mammon, technology, politics, religiosity) and submit to other gods (forms, success, prestige, "growth") in questions of worship,[59] so it is not necessary to add much here. It is not success or growth, of course, that is inherently wrong. The problem arises when these goals overstep their bounds and become gods (fallen powers), when they cause us to trust ourselves and our strategies instead of knowing our weakness through which the power of God tabernacles.

Furthermore, it has probably been obvious throughout the preceding sections of this chapter that all the facets of the community's Christian life are intertwined with its worship in a spiraling cause-and-effect dialectic. For example, the god mammon disturbs worship (when people care more for the clothes they are wearing and the impression they are making than for God, let's say), which in turn causes the worship service to be less capable of forming a community that lives by economic redistribution, which in turn triggers more corruption by mammon's influence on both the members and the corporate community.

Nevertheless, by means of an Australian slant a few comments can be added here to reinforce points I've made elsewhere. One aspect of worship decisions that exemplifies a "fallen powers" influence is the problem that vocabulary is often contorted, with unbiblical results in our choices. In the following excerpt, social commentator Hugh Mackay makes a wise observation that churches should consider:

> It's clear from these concerns that we must constantly remind ourselves — and we must remind our children — about the difference between machines and people. For a start, we should delete the term "user-friendly" from our vocabulary! Machines may be easy or difficult to use, but they are neither friendly nor unfriendly. Machines may be quick, accurate and convenient, but they do not possess such qualities as courage, integrity, fidelity or moral sensitivity. Machines are not patient, generous or tolerant. Those are qualities which peo-

---

59. See Marva J. Dawn, *Reaching Out without Dumbing Down: A Theology of Worship for This Urgent Time* (Grand Rapids: Wm. B. Eerdmans Publishing Co., 1995), and *A Royal "Waste" of Time: The Splendor of Worshiping God and Being Church for the World* (Grand Rapids: Wm. B. Eerdmans Publishing Co., 1999).

ple possess, and those are the very qualities which are fundamental to the whole process of human communication.[60]

Often churches choose to discard hymnbooks, liturgies, symbols, and practices of worship because they are claimed to be not as user-friendly. Inanimate objects are not the issue — the people are!

Lack of genuine hospitality is the issue; failure to be witnesses to, or lovers of, our neighbors is the problem. In *A Royal "Waste" of Time*, I offer several chapters exploring this matter. Let me simply summarize here that it is a function of fallen powers that we do not discern the true problem and merely apply a quick-fix Technique in the attempt to make our church popular and "attractive" (which also are false gods). The point of public worship is corporate praise of God, not private coziness or the satisfaction of our personal desires. We fail our true vocation when our churches cater to such self-centeredness. And we usually do that out of a desire for success, to attract numbers — which, again, is to act as a fallen power rather than a faithful one. Weakness chooses the tougher road — to give people in worship what will keep the focus on God, form our character, and nurture the kind of community that will — in weakness — display the tabernacling of God and not ourselves.

All this is related to another comment by Hugh Mackay that grabbed my attention. He gives the example of the death of the television series "Lois and Clark."

> The market research won: give the viewers what they *say* they want (almost always a very different thing from what they actually want). So the decision was made to let Lois and Superman/Clark marry. The result — do I really need to tell you? — was that the program's popularity plummeted and, soon after, the series was canceled by the American ABC network. (133)

Why do churches give people what they *say* they want and not what they really need? Similarly,

> In more recent politics, there has been an ugly development: the emergence of the opinion poll as a substitute for leadership. Let the

---

60. Mackay, *Turning Point*, p. 242. Page references to this book in the following paragraphs will be given parenthetically in the text.

polls tell me what people want to hear, and that's what I'll say. Let the polls tell me what I can get away with, and that's how far I'll go. Let the polls tell me how to be popular, and I'll be all those things. (134)

The same ugly development has taken over worship discussions (as it has politics, especially in election years). The opinion poll is the substitute for genuine theological and musical leadership. When will we learn that the newest and most popular is not always the best vehicle (nor is the old, necessarily) to carry the eternal, the character forming, the authentic praise of all the people with all our best and sacrificial gifts?

Personal opinions are not God. "Growing" congregations are not God. Charismatic pastors and winsome worship leaders are not God. Church buildings are not God. Worship forms and musical styles are not God. Numbers are not God. Educational programs are not God. Service projects are not God, nor are women's groups, youth groups, church councils, or stewardship schemes. The vocation of all of these is to praise God in the Trinity's absolute sovereignty and sympathy, mercy and might. If any of the above move away from that calling, it is idolatry, a case of fallen powers.

People object, "But our congregation might decline if we don't use new music" (or whatever else becomes an idolatry). So??? The issue is not whether one's numbers stay up. The issue is for what reason they are declining. Is it a lack of hospitality, a loss of focus, a rejection of the Church's true calling, a failure to make Christ's presence known? *Of course* we should use new music — but only if it praises God better (which it often does!).

The Challenge

One more observation by Hugh Mackay causes me great anguish and spurs me to passion. In his chapter on "Spirituality . . . or Sports," he suggests, "Given the extent and depth of Australians' doubts and uncertainties, the present time might be considered ripe for a revival of religious faith and practice. But the signs do not seem to be pointing in that direction" (219). Too many other powers prevent the much-needed revival in most of the wealthy nations of the world. There is too much subjectivism to recognize our need for substantive doctrinal foundations, too much sexual pleasure and too many internetted multi-relationships to distract us from our need for genuine fellowship, too much luxury to enjoy a simple feast of bread and wine, too much politics to be engaged in to pray, too much technology by which to be dazzled, too much mammon to be gained, too many other gods to waste our time worshiping the crucified Christ — in short, too many competing powers for people to realize that what they long for most of all is to worship God and to be weak so that trinitarian tabernacling could ensue.

What shall we do? I pray that this chapter has convinced you that the answer is not to resort to techniques of power. Johann Christoph Blumhardt (1805-1880), about whom we read in the first chapter, offers another possibility.

When the awakening in Möttlingen, Germany (where the congregation had formerly been afflicted with a crippling spiritual lethargy), began to ebb because the villagers were quite overworked by it all, Blumhardt observed and wrote,

> Many weaknesses of human nature — weaknesses one might hardly take into account, but which have deep significance if our Christianity is not to consist of mere fragments — became apparent to me. I recognized such weaknesses in myself first, and following an inner urge, confessed them to one of my colleagues. I felt humbled by my shortcomings, omissions, stupidities, and bad habits — and from then on I sat on the same bench with my congregation. I did this by bringing my failings before them, and the result was the emergence of a new movement of repentance and humility. Once more my parishioners searched their souls and, for the most part, sought me out again.

Günter Krüger's introduction goes on with this account:

> It should be noted — especially today, when there is a wealth of theories on how to revitalize dying churches — that Blumhardt had no such strategies at hand. He applied himself vigorously in rebuilding his parish, yet he always maintained that the master builder was God. He also observed something seldom mentioned today in discussions of spiritual renewal: the problem of believers who, though respectable and sincerely committed, are influenced or even bound by forces of darkness. In retrospect, he noted that these forces presented the

greatest obstacle to renewal in his parish. As long as the reality of satanic power was not recognized, exposed, and done away with in every corner, the suffocating spiritual fog that hung over the church would not lift.

Modern minds tend to deny or ignore the very existence of satanic forces, let alone their hold on specific individuals. Blumhardt felt that this skepticism trivializes the reality of evil. He argued that every human being has demons of his or her own to fight, that all are affected in some way by the power of evil. . . .

Blumhardt saw the kingdom of God as a state from which all forces hostile to God would be banished in the aggressive battle that must be fought against 'the prince of this world.' The church, Blumhardt said, must take part in this offensive and to do so successfully it must call on divine authority.

If Blumhardt is right, it follows that the Christian's life must take on the character of a war. Today the church does not face merely one possessed woman [the church member Gottlieben], but a world infected and overrun with demons in the most varied spheres — politics, technology, economics, academia, religion, and art. And unless we recognize and identify these demons, the spheres under their sway can not serve the cause of God.

For followers of Jesus, then, the challenge is to take leave of all spiritual pacifism, all egotistical and self-centered private piety. It means mobilizing and taking to the front lines.[61]

This witness is extremely pertinent to our times. Blumhardt's avoidance of curiosity in dealing with powers of evil, his recognition of the unmet needs of thousands for pastoral care, his yearning to transform the "wretched state" of Christian life, and his fervent prayers for a fresh outpouring of the Spirit are all needed today.

To be Christian churches is to resist being swept up into the values and powers of our cultural milieu. On the other hand, the role of the Christian community is to supply what is missing in that milieu — namely, the tabernacling of Christ. The sole meaning of the preaching of

61. Overview by Günter Krüger, in Friedrich Zuendel, *The Awakening: One Man's Battle with Darkness* (Farmington, PA: The Plough Publishing House, 1999), pp. 10-12, 18-19.

the gospel is that others might know the grace that is available in Jesus Christ. However, this can happen only if God's people first give up their own workings of power in order to receive the tabernacling of God in our weakness.

Most of this chapter can be summarized as a warning lest churches forget their own theology of the cross and adopt the methods of the world, instead of remembering their unique role in relation to the powers. We must always keep in mind that the Greek word *methodia* is used only twice in the New Testament (Eph. 4:14 and 6:11) — and both times pejoratively. Discovering that has caused me to be more careful always to question my "methods," to ask if they are God's or those of fallen powers. As G. B. Caird emphasizes, the Church must remember, in fulfilling its tasks in relation to the powers, that the divinely created authorities have become instruments of evil. To think that evil can be defeated by any of these agencies — "by the action of the state, by the self-discipline of the conscience, or by the processes of nature" — "is to ask that Satan cast out Satan." The powers can be stripped of their tyrannical influence and restored to their proper subjection to God "only in the Cross."[62]

Once again I close the chapter with devotional selections for further pondering. All of the chapter's themes — the temptations of the powers; our weakness and the possibility of God's tabernacling; the weakness of Christ; and the life of the Christian community through Christ's Spirit — can be found in this hymn by Brian Wren and this reading from Russian Orthodox writer Sergei Fudel (1901-1977):

"Great God, Your Love Has Called Us Here"

Great God, your love has called us here as we, by love,
    for love were made.
Your living likeness still we bear, though marred,
    dishonored, disobeyed.
We come, with all our heart and mind your call to hear,
    your love to find.

We come with self-inflicted pains of broken trust and chosen wrong,
half-free, half-bound by inner chains, by social forces swept along,

---

62. G. B. Caird, *Principalities and Powers: A Study in Pauline Theology* (Oxford: Clarendon Press, 1956), p. 101.

by pow'rs and systems close confined yet seeking hope
    for humankind.

Great God, in Christ you call our name and then receive us
    as your own
not through some merit, right, or claim but by your
    gracious love alone.
We strain to glimpse your mercy seat and find you kneeling
    at our feet.

Then take the towel, and break the bread, and humble us,
    and call us friends.
Suffer and serve till all are fed and show how grandly love intends
to work till all creation sings, to fill all worlds, to crown all things.

Great God, in Christ you set us free your life to live, your joy to share.
Give us your Spirit's liberty to turn from guilt and dull despair
and offer all that faith can do while love is making all things new.[63]

A Reading for the Day after Ash Wednesday

Along with the immortal life of Christ's Church, evil has always
existed, within the very enclosure of the Church. We must see this
with our eyes open, always remembering that "the hand in the dish
with Me, will betray Me." Saint Chrysostom was not afraid to recognize the spiritual sickness within his local church and to speak of it.
Father John of Kronstadt said: "Unless you learn to recognize the
spirit that kills, you will not learn to know the lifegiving Spirit. Only
through the contrast of good and evil, of life and death, do we learn
to understand both." And just now our Church lives through a time
when it is especially important for Christians to clearly understand
both life and death.

Father Valentine Sventitsky was in many ways a typical Russian,
married priest, but he was also a real teacher of constant prayer. As
early as 1925, right in the middle of Moscow, his sermons were a call

---

63. Brian Wren, © 1975, 1995 Hope Publishing Co., Carol Stream, IL 60188. All
rights reserved. Used by permission. Sing to the tune ABINGDON, Erik Routley
(1945); #579 in the Moravian Hymnal.

to constant spiritual effort. He defended faith, but his greatest message was this constant call to prayer, to the burning life of the spirit. "Prayer builds walls around our monastery in the world," he used to say.

Summing up the problem of sin within the Church he said: "A sin within the Church is not sin of the Church, but against the Church." Breaking away from the Church because of the moral derelictions we see in it is religiously foolish and reflects our inability to think things through. Anything wrong, distorted and impure that we see within the gates of the Church is not the Church. To avoid associating with it we do not have to leave the Church enclosure, we must simply refuse to participate in that which is evil. Then will be fulfilled the words "to the pure all things are pure" ([Titus] 1:15).[64]

64. Sergei Fudel, from *Light in the Darkness*, quoted in *For All the Saints*, pp. 777-78.

4 What, Then, Shall the Church Be? Images of Weakness

We have seen the pervasiveness of fallen powers overstepping their bounds in our world (Chapter 1). We have traced the vigorously consistent picture suffusing all of the Scriptures showing that, instead of acting out of its own power, the Church is to live by its weakness imbued with the tabernacling of God (Chapter 2). And we have looked at many ways in which churches lose track of that biblical orientation and function instead according to different visions and by different methods and powers (Chapter 3). In light of all this, many questions, such as the following, are raised (though not all can be thoroughly addressed in this chapter):

If the Triune God tabernacles in our weakness, what does the corporate weakness of the Christian community look like?

How can a congregation fulfill its call to weakness as a power true to its vocation?

How will personal weakness affect the corporate, and vice versa?

Is it possible for a church denomination to operate out of weakness? Is it really possible for a congregation to do so?

How do we, in a theology of weakness, avoid passivity? resignation? apathy?

If fallen powers are so pervasive and if even churches always act somewhat from fallenness, is there hope anywhere? What will it mean for us to resist, confound, and stand against the powers?

One thing we can know for sure at the outset: We can't simply float along, as Miroslav Volf insists in a *Christian Century* article. He describes a religiously and politically conservative family who "created an alternative culture" — alternative to society, as well as to the lives of many Christians. In these times such people are the true "radicals," rather than the political left of past decades. About the rest of us Volf complains,

> Instead of purposefully walking to determinate places, we are aim-
> lessly floating with random currents. Of course, we do get exercised
> by issues and engage in bitter feuds over them. But that makes us
> even less capable of resisting the pull of the larger culture, a resis-
> tance that would take shape in formulating and embodying a coher-
> ent alternative way of life.[1]

Jacques Ellul issued the same call for deliberate alternativity in 1948 in the French edition of his first major theological book, *The Presence of the Kingdom.* This book still gives eminently timely — and timeless — instructions for being the Church in weakness for the sake of God's tabernacling in and through us. In its second paragraph, the book reminds us (as we always need to be re-reminded) of the requirement that the Christian be *in* the world, but not *of* it. Ellul insists that

> This means that his thought, his life, and his heart are not controlled
> by the world, and do not depend upon the world, for they belong to
> another Master. Thus, since he belongs to another Master, the Chris-
> tian has been sent into this world by this Master, and his communion
> with his Master remains unbroken, in spite of the "world" in which
> he has to live.
>
> But this communion of the Christian with Jesus Christ has some
> serious implications: first of all, the Christian, by this very fact, finds
> that he is not confronted by the material forces of the world but by its
> spiritual reality. Because he is in communion with Jesus Christ he has
> to fight not against flesh and blood but against "the principalities,
> against the powers, against the world-rulers of this darkness." At the
> same time this communion assures him that he does not belong to
> the world, that he is free from the fatality of the world which is mov-
> ing towards death, and, as a result of this liberation by grace, he *can*

1. Miroslav Volf, "Faith Matters: Floating Along?" *Christian Century* 117, no. 11 (5 April 2000): 398.

fight against the spiritual realities of the world. To speak quite plainly, he is called to break the fatality which hangs over the world, and he *can* do so.[2]

Ellul summarizes the functions of Christians with these three biblical passages:

1. You are the salt of the earth.
2. You are the light of the world.
3. I send you forth as sheep in the midst of wolves. (9)

Citing Leviticus 2:13, he emphasizes that the salt is the "sign" of the covenant between God and Israel. Similarly, Christians are to be the visible sign of the new covenant that God made with the world through Jesus Christ (9). The work of light is to eliminate darkness, to give the criterion of goodness. The light also "gives meaning and direction to the history of the world, and thus explains it" (10). The third description, sheep in the midst of wolves, again points to the Christian as a "sign" of the reality of God's action. Every Christian is

> treated like his Master, and every Christian receives from Jesus Christ a share in His work. He is a "sheep" not because his action or his sacrifice has a purifying effect on the world, but because he is the living and real "sign," constantly renewed in the midst of the world, of the sacrifice of the Lamb of God. In the world everyone wants to be a "wolf," and no one is called to play the part of a "sheep." Yet the world cannot *live* without this living witness of sacrifice. That is why it is essential that Christians should be very careful not to be "wolves" in the spiritual sense — that is, people who try to dominate others. Christians must accept the domination of other people, and offer the daily sacrifice of their lives, which is united with the sacrifice of Jesus Christ. (11)[3]

2. Jacques Ellul, *The Presence of the Kingdom*, trans. Olive Wyon (New York: Seabury Press, 1967), pp. 7-8. Page references to this book in the following paragraphs will be given parenthetically in the text.

3. It is interesting to compare these early comments from Ellul on violence and sacrifice with the powerfully insightful work of René Girard, especially *Violence and the*

Ellul's comments reiterate what we discovered in Chapter 3 about being in our weakness a sacrament, a sign — incarnating God's truth instead of human opinions, living in a fellowship of vulnerability and forgiveness instead of power, breaking down all power barriers between people in the community, breaking the bread of suffering gladly because we taste Christ's suffering on our behalf in our life together, feasting on the eucharist as a sign of Christ's defeat of the principalities and powers, enduring by prayer instead of politics and discerning by that prayer God's means for acting in political situations that we encounter, pointing to God's signs and wonders by boasting of nothing but our own weakness, knowing our own poverty and thereby being freed to desacralize mammon and to offer our mercy with a view toward economic redistribution in the world, and worshiping God alone — thereby dethroning all other idolatries and powers.

As we noted in Chapter 1, Christ's victory over the powers on the cross was decisive, but the battle against them must continue through time, since the powers rage in their struggle to be emancipated. In this chapter, let's consider how from our weakness the Church will engage in the battle by taking up the panoply or armor of God described for us in Ephesians 6.

We take up this panoply with great courage and Joy because it is God's panoply. As illuminated by Hendrik Berkhof's illustration of the "hunger winter" in the Netherlands in 1944-45 after the Nazis had been defeated but while they were still oppressing the Dutch,[4] there has been a change in the objective reality of the powers. Since the powers' sovereignty has been broken and a limit has been set to their working, the Church, clothed in God's armor, is the sign and the promise of their ultimate and total defeat.

Because it is God's panoply, the Church's stance is very different from that of the world around it. In an extensive listing of aspects of this stance, Jacques Ellul includes these elements among others:

Sacred, trans. Patrick Gregory (Baltimore: Johns Hopkins University Press, 1977); *The Scapegoat,* trans. Yvonne Freccero (Baltimore: Johns Hopkins University Press, 1986); and *Things Hidden Since the Foundation of the World,* trans. Stephen Bann and Michael Metteer (Stanford: Stanford University Press, 1987). See also Jacques Ellul's principal book on the subject, *Violence: Reflections from a Christian Perspective,* trans. Cecelia Gaul Kings (New York: Seabury Press, 1969), and Willard M. Swartley, ed., *Violence Renounced: René Girard, Biblical Studies, and Peacemaking,* vol. 4 of *Studies in Peace and Scripture* (Telford, PA: Pandora Press U.S., 2000).

4. This example was introduced in Chapter 1 and is found in Hendrik Berkhof, *Christ and the Powers,* trans. John H. Yoder (Scottdale, PA: Herald Press, 1962), p. 43.

"The Church's stance can only result from a future now in process."[5]

"The Church is called to speak on the basis of revelation, not on the basis of the happenings and proddings of the world" (178).

The Church will experience a permanent tension with respect to the world (178-82).

"The Church and Christians have to take as their starting point revelation, the Gospel. . . . She should base herself on that which makes her the Church, that is, on her election by God, and on the revelation committed to her as a precious deposit" (182-83).

The Church should concern herself with world problems larger than current phenomena, with an active presence against various powers like money, technology, etc. (184-86).

In that role the Church could exercise a genuine prophetic ministry (187-90) and the ministries of reconciliation (190-98) and aid (198-202).

The pastor bears the image of the Reconciler himself (192).

"But, in the very degree to which the Church and Christians are witnesses to the one true God who has revealed himself, they have the stern duty of desacralization and demystification to perform in society" (202-3).

All divinizations should be ruthlessly destroyed: "We have to reject the sacred of work, of technology, of science, of production. It is, above all else, a matter of spiritual combat." Scripture is the true destroyer of myths (204-8).

The Church's task is to open up the world, particularly to God and especially since the world tries to exclude God (208-10).

Bearing these dimensions of our stance in mind, let us turn to the armor of God catalogued in Ephesians 6. Because the corporate life of the Church's communities and the individual lives of Christian believers are constantly intertwined and influencing each other, I will mix my examples. Sometimes the example of one leader is sufficient to influence an entire community (for good or ill, fallenness or faithfulness). I must emphasize, though, that my primary goal in this book is that our *churches* could be vital communities exhibiting God's strength in our weakness.

5. Jacques Ellul, *False Presence of the Kingdom*, trans. C. Edward Hopkin (New York: Seabury Press, 1972), p. 178. Page references to the following points from this book will be given parenthetically in the text.

The Divine Warrior Is God

It might seem that I should have chosen the weapons of the panoply in Ephesians to discuss resisting the powers in Chapter 3 and the vision of Acts 2 for this chapter's description of the faithful Church, but I reversed that apparent logic for three main reasons.

First, living in the grace-full paradox of power through weakness is a tough dialectic; it requires constant practice to reorganize our thinking, so I tried to throw our usual categories into an unnatural pattern to help us exercise thinking on God's slant.

Second, elsewhere in the Scriptures weakness and warfare are combined, and the contrast heightens the point. In 2 Corinthians Paul responds to criticism that his behavior in person is very different from the tone of his letters. Timothy Savage describes Paul's strategy:

> Knowing that a display of visible force would, far from winning the obedience of his converts, actually prolong their human boasting and lead them ultimately to destruction, he comes to them in a premeditated spirit of meekness and gentleness. That is not to say that he comes without boldness. On the contrary, it is precisely in such "weakness" that he intends to engage in bold warfare, tearing down strongholds and taking captive the self-exalting attitudes which come into conflict with the knowledge of God (10:3-6).[6]

Third, as will be elaborated below, Tom Yoder Neufeld radically reoriented my thinking by demonstrating that the panoply of God's armor is offensive and not just defensive, as we are usually taught.[7] This fits more strongly with my urging that Christians be more active as creative agents of God's kingdom — sentinels on the wall instead of late responders, proactive agents instead of reactive ones, dynamic recipients and transmitters of God's power rather than wielders of our own power falsely exer-

6. Timothy B. Savage, *Power Through Weakness: Paul's Understanding of the Christian Ministry in 2 Corinthians,* Society for New Testament Studies Monograph Series 86 (Cambridge: Cambridge University Press, 1996), p. 69.

7. See Thomas R. Yoder Neufeld, *'Put on the Armour of God': The Divine Warrior from Isaiah to Ephesians,* Journal for the Study of the New Testament Supplement Series 140 (Sheffield, England: Sheffield Academic Press, 1997), and also his *Ephesians,* Believers Church Bible Commentary (Scottdale, PA: Herald Press, forthcoming).

cised or wimpy forgetters of our gospel vocation. God's armor is not a secure haven in which to hide — in Harvey Cox's image of circling the
wagons in fundamentalist fear — but, on the other side, neither does it
permit a "collage" of spirituality, with bits and pieces from various traditions.[8] Not in such extremes of shutting out the world or of sampling every
kind of spirituality the world offers will God's presence be found.

To know God's presence and power for resistance against, and defeat
of, the principalities requires that we wear and utilize the specific equipment God offers. In our weakness, we cannot combat the powers; we could
never be capable of the engagement. We *must* be equipped with God's panoply, with God himself. Undergirding my discussion of this armor is Tom
Yoder Neufeld's survey of the Divine Warrior imagery in the Bible, in
which he makes pressingly clear how much the battle is the Lord's.[9]

Using the panoply for our positive view of the Church operating out of
weakness is helpful especially if we keep in mind the rest of the letter to the
Ephesians, which is certainly one of the richest books in the New Testament in its emphasis on grace. In his forthcoming commentary, Yoder
Neufeld captures this emphasis succinctly:

> The church lives in the eschatological moment, *buying out the time*
> (5:16 . . .), which, it turns out, implies taking the struggle to heal the
> cosmos to its very edges. . . . To be sure, the church does not displace
> God. After all, for the church to be the body of God's Messiah (1:23),
> for it to possess the fullness of God (1:23, 3:19), for believers to be
> raised and seated in the heavenlies together with the Messiah (2:5,6),
> is first and last the result of God's grace (2:8-10). Human pride and
> accomplishment are absolutely excluded (2:9).[10]

Being Strong in the Lord's Power

The description of the battle against the principalities and powers in Ephesians 6 begins with this utter dependence upon grace, upon God's

8. Harvey Cox, professor at Harvard Divinity School, in a "Weekend Edition" inter-
view with Scott Simon on National Public Radio, January 1, 2000.

9. Yoder Neufeld, *'Put on the Armour of God,'* pp. 131-45.

10. Yoder Neufeld, *Ephesians,* manuscript p. 402.

strength, upon the Lord's tabernacling in Triune armor. Verse 10 offers a plea with three different Greek words for being "strong in the Lord and in the strength of his power" *(endunamoō, kratos, ischus)*.

The battle is not only totally dependent upon God, but it is also local as well as cosmic, a resistance of evil powers in daily life, particularly in the corporate lives of our churches. Putting on the armor is not the work of individual Christians so much as that of the whole Body of the Church. The verb form from *endunamoō* is a second person plural imperative, so it literally commands, "be empowered, all y'all" as my Southern friends would say.

Until reading Tom Yoder Neufeld's work I was hesitant to use the armor of God as a means for thinking about the Church's positive role as a created power that remembers its weakness — primarily because I have always been taught and thought that the weapons of the panoply were entirely defensive except for the sword. Consequently, I thought that this metaphor would reinforce many churches' culturally induced passivity, the "Low Information-Action Ratio" that Neil Postman bemoans. I was also concerned about using imagery that might suggest violence, when the stance of weakness is one that counters the powers of violence.

But Yoder Neufeld taught me (1) to think of the panoply as offensive through the detailed comparisons of Divine Warrior imagery in his dissertation, (2) that the emphasis in the biblical text is more on the virtues and actions than on the pieces of equipment in the metaphor, and (3) that the military imagery does not promote war mongering if we remember its critical irony.

"The powers are vanquished," Yoder Neufeld writes, "through the exercise of truth, justice, peace, and liberation, just as they are through the exercise of the word and prayer."[11] These are all practices, virtues, and actions that remain our focus because they are the weapons of the Divine Warrior. God's methods, not the elements of the armor, carry the metaphor.

If we accentuate the weaponry, we lose the metaphor's irony and risk aligning ourselves with our culture's militarism, which, as one example of the general enmity Christ has overcome (see Eph. 2:16), is one of the powers against which we stand to expose, disarm, and overcome it. As Yoder Neufeld urges us, "The critical and *essential* task is to maintain the irony in

11. Yoder Neufeld, *Ephesians*, manuscript p. 408. Page references to this manuscript in the following paragraphs will be given parenthetically in the text.

such warfare, and to remain deeply conscious that this is always a battle *for blood and flesh* and never ever *against* it" (428).

There are thus two essential paradoxes to be kept in mind throughout this chapter. The first is that to counteract the principalities and powers requires a battle, but one that is essentially and entirely nonviolent because it is against the powers and never against the people who might be aligned with them. The second is that the battle requires our active engagement, but it is always God's work through our weakness.

This weakness stance is well illustrated by the comments of a group of twenty-three ethicists and peace activists who gathered for a working conference at the Carter Center. One of the members, Ted Koontz, said that "he had moved from 'this world is a mess and I need to fix it' to 'God is moving in history to do something, and I can join in.' The result of their work is the book *Just Peacemaking,* which describes what the conference members "see God doing in our history so that people can join in." Three of them note in their introduction,

> Some Christians resist, expressing fatalism. They cite the book of Revelation to support their belief that we cannot spread peacemaking. We should not hope to reduce or eliminate war, they say, because the Bible says there will be wars and rumors of war. We believe this misreads the message of the book of Revelation. Throughout the biblical drama, we are taught that though the powers and authorities seem in control, God is sovereign; and we are to be faithful to God's teachings. This is also the message of the book of Revelation: God is the real ruler; God is judging the powers who seem to be ruling for now and who are causing wars. God will redeem the followers of the Lamb; therefore, do not lose hope; follow the teachings of the Lamb. The followers of the Lamb do the deeds Jesus teaches. The same point is repeated again and again in varieties of phrasing, so often that one wonders how people could miss it. The followers of the Lamb are those who do the deeds Jesus teaches, who do God's will, keep God's Word, keep God's commandments, hold faithful to the testimony of Jesus, do the teachings of Jesus, follow God's teachings as given through Jesus, obey God's commands (Rev. 2:2; 2:23; 2:19; 2:26; 3:8, 10; 9:20-21; 12:17; 14:4; 14:12; 16:11; 19:10; 20:12-13; 22:11).[12]

12. Duane K. Friesen, John Langan, S.J., Glen Stassen, "Introduction: Just Peace-

As with peacemaking, so with all the dimensions in our following the Lamb. This is the major paradox of the Christian life: in our *active* weakness, God's power is at work through us. Faithfulness is required, but success is not.

Effectiveness Does Not Matter

In asking if weakness means passivity, we have discovered that it means instead a rigorous battle in which we remember that the armor with which we fight and the victory we win are the Lord's. Now we must ask if weakness is an effective or ineffective way to be the Church. The answer to that question takes several forms.

First, I think the word *effective* has led many churches astray. Because our goal is that God's power and purposes might be at work through our weakness, we can concentrate not on the results, but on the means in the very gifts of God's tabernacling. The book of Ephesians shows that agency, as Yoder Neufeld points out, with its

> very marked interest in wisdom (1:8, 17-23; 3:10, 14-19; 5:15-17), in nonconformity (4:17–5:17), and in worship (1:3-14; 3:14-21; 5:18-21). And it stresses the *practical* and *communal* exercise of truth, justice, peace, and the word of God, and finally prayer, so as to enable believers to preach the good news (6:14-20), which in Ephesians is most centrally the overcoming of enmity *within the human community.* In Ephesians the greatest evidence of the demonic lies in the existence of disobedience of God's will for humanity (2:1-10), in the hostile and exclusionary divisions within the human community (2:11-22; 3:1-13), and in the darkness of a culture blind to the gravity of license, greed, and falsity (4:17–5:21). We know, as does the author of Ephesians, that the larger culturally experienced forces are the chief culprits in nurturing such hostilities. That is precisely why the alternative cultural forces of truth, justice, and peace are so important. When these are "wielded" by a community that is "in Christ" — that has put on the "new human" — then its very life is "exorcistic." (466-67)

---

making as a New Ethic," in *Just Peacemaking: Ten Practices for Abolishing War,* ed. Glen Stassen (Cleveland: Pilgrim Press, 1998), p. 21.

The Church's call is to exorcism, rather than effectiveness. Perhaps one of the most recalcitrant spirits that needs to be exorcized is that of needing to be effective.[13]

However, I hastily add as my second point that often the Church's faithfulness does indeed lead to efficacy. Lee Earl describes as follows what happened when his congregation responded to the death of a mother gunned down across the street from the church building:

> When Twelfth Street Baptist Church began to reach out to the community after Alice's death, we did not set out to reduce crime. That was not our original mission. We hoped to establish, maintain, and demonstrate the presence of God in the midst of that community and to do what the Lord had called us to do. What we discovered in the process is that in doing ministry the way that Jesus commanded, we had an impact on crime. The church that lives out the teaching of Jesus Christ has the ability to have a concrete, quantifiable, measurable impact on improving quality of life in the community.[14]

The key, obviously, is not to ask about effectiveness, but to ask how to wield the armor of God. Then effectiveness is a lovely surprise, a great gift to the community, a stunning reminder that in our weakness the battle is the Lord's.

Third, the same faithfulness that frees us from questions about effectiveness also delivers us from worries about the location of our engagement in struggles against the powers. Mother Teresa showed us perhaps more clearly than anyone the relationship between obedience in weakness and the discipleship of ministry. "When asked about how God had called her to work amongst the poor, she replied that God had not called her to work among the poor. He called her to follow him and led her there."[15]

13. See chapter 2, "Ceasing Productivity and Accomplishment," in Marva J. Dawn, *Keeping the Sabbath Wholly: Ceasing, Resting, Embracing, Feasting* (Grand Rapids: Wm. B. Eerdmans Publishing Co., 1989), pp. 17-21.

14. Lee A. Earl, "The Spiritual Problem of Crime: A Pastor's Call," in *God and the Victim: Theological Reflections on Evil, Victimization, Justice, and Forgiveness,* ed. Lisa Barnes Lampman and Michelle Shattuck (Grand Rapids: Wm. B. Eerdmans Publishing Co., 1999), p. 246.

15. Quoted from *God So Loves the City: Seeking a Theology for Urban Mission* in

Finally, the question of faithfulness versus effectiveness is put in right perspective by Bill Wylie Kellermann's reference to "the bloody denouement of the eucharistic image." In light of that image, he asks, "Ought our first concern [to] be deeds which generate immediate and visible results? Or should it rather be unerring fidelity to conscience and the gospel?" His emphasis on liturgical actions offers a certain resolution of this dilemma.

The Church is first called to worship the true God, to desacralize all other powers. Wylie Kellermann offers some examples of Christian groups who have undertaken specific liturgical actions at missile bases or in the face of economic oppression, or elsewhere, and he concludes that

> symbolic struggle is real struggle, that liturgy can effectively subvert or resist or even transform a political situation, that the world-making power of liturgy is a real force of social construction. On the other hand, liturgical actions exhibit what Gandhi called "non-attachment to results." Since their intention is not firstly instrumental, but always toward God as gift and offering, they permit a tremendous freedom. One would never ask of a eucharist: Was it successful or effective? It simply is.[16]

I would like to widen his comment to give us a vision for all the Church's worshipful life (in doctrine, fellowship, breaking of bread, and so forth). Let us not ask of our actions or way of life in the armor of God whether we are effective; let us simply BE. Are we, in our weakness, truly being the locus of tabernacling?

Let us turn now to particular elements of the panoply by which we engage in the battle that is not against flesh and blood, but against the principalities and rulers, "against the cosmic powers of this present darkness, against the spiritual forces of evil in the heavenly places" (Eph. 6:12). We take up this panoply so that we "may be able to withstand on that evil day, and having done everything, to stand firm" (v. 13). As in Chapter 3, we will discover that all the elements of the armor work together, intertwining their functions and effects, influencing each other in a continuous spiral.

Harold Dean Trulear, "Go and Do Likewise: The Church's Role in Caring for Crime Victims," in Lampman and Shattuck, eds., *God and the Victim*, p. 75.

16. Bill Wylie Kellermann, *Seasons of Faith and Conscience: Kairos, Confession, Liturgy* (Maryknoll, NY: Orbis Books, 1991), p. 128.

The Belt of Truth

How might the Church in all its weakness wield truth or trustworthiness in our "age of the lie"? How might we demonstrate that, unseen by human beings but infinitely real, there are other dimensions to every situation which are unknown to us, that there is a truth above and beyond the visible alternatives?

First, we will wield truth in our doctrine by holding fast to a theology of the cross, not merely as a principle, but as the center of our life as Church. We preach nothing but Christ crucified and raised again. If we teach and demonstrate Christ's cross thoroughly in our churches in all its ramifications of weakness, then we are more likely to form in members a way of life that operates out of weakness, and we are more likely to live with each other in suffering servanthood.

This is certainly not what is being taught in a congregation whose billboard recently proclaimed, "After a week like the one you've had, you deserve a Sunday like we have." What does that say about the church and its core theology? Such marketing verbalizes a theology of myself — that I have *earned* the gifts of faith, that worship is to cater to my desires for comfort and entertainment. One would hardly come to such a "deserved" Sunday to be equipped for mission, to remember the cross, to acknowledge our idolatries. This church offers products for consumption, just like the groceries my husband was on his way to buy when he saw that sign.

To put on God's truth is to wield the Triune way of weakness throughout all seven of the practices in the Acts 2 vision, which, as we saw in the previous chapter, are thoroughly intertwined. A theology of the cross as the core of our doctrine will imbue our fellowship, breaking of bread, prayers, signs and wonders, economic redistribution, and worship with a sense of Christ's weakness and, thereby, more richly, of our own.

The truth of the cross, of weakness, affects our doctrinal methods, too. We will not resort to the power of "historical proof" in modernist terms, or to postmodern nihilistic deconstruction of texts, but we will submit in weakness to texts and ask how God might use them to form us, and we will glory in being a community trusting the power of the Holy Spirit and the faithfulness of our forebears. Instead of resorting to a hermeneutics of suspicion, we will look for the presence of Christ tabernacling in his Word and in his Body as the living Jesus.

Beyond speaking and living truth in its own doctrine and internal practices, how does the Church wield truth in its relations with the world? If we are to be faithful to our position in weakness, we will know that we offer truth best not by pontificating pronouncements or political maneuverings, but by simply speaking and living truly.

In *The Humiliation of the Word,* written in 1981, Jacques Ellul catalogs ways in which our culture's forces/powers destroy veracity by contempt for language, hatred of the word, and *de facto* devaluation (through continued talking when one has nothing to say, intellectual "logorrhea," and excessive information, which is a specific result of the increasing technologization of society).[17] Then, in a closing ethical coda for Christians, Ellul offers guidance for dealing with the destruction of language in our technological society.

Under his first point, which is the command of iconoclasm (that is, to oppose or destroy false religious images), he includes such practical suggestions as combating the worship of television, the reduction of thought in audiovisuals, and even the hypnotic effects of computer terminals (256). Obviously, he is not opposed to technical advances nor to images, which are legitimate, useful, sometimes even necessary for life, but he especially emphasizes that Christians must "oppose their imperialism and pride, the covetousness and spirit of conquest they inspire, and their pretension to be without limits" (259).

Ellul's second category of suggestions relates to restoring reality to its proper limits. He warns against attacking images that are "reduced to their proper level, function, and role" and commends the value of aesthetic expression. The problem arises, however, when images claim to bear all of truth (259). Then they must be restored to their authenticity (260).

Next, Ellul posits the need for comprehensible language and urges Christians to be rigorous and precise in their use of it. Furthermore, language must be used to "construct, exhort, and console" and must be clearly understood if it will succeed in those functions (260-61). Jesus offers a model of using "reasonable language, as the perfect vehicle for the absolute Word." Another part of the Christian task is to "challenge energetically all the snares and temptations of mysterious, mystical, delirious, and fiery language" (263). (This comment is especially useful if reread frequently during U.S. presidential campaigns and during church debates.)

---

17. Jacques Ellul, *The Humiliation of the Word,* trans. Joyce Main Hanks (Grand Rapids: Wm. B. Eerdmans Publishing Co., 1985), pp. 155-82. Page references to this book in the following discussion are given parenthetically in the text.

Finally, Ellul stresses the importance of open language (not closed by repetition or redundancy), and he suggests that political, scientific, ideological, and catechetical forms of discourse often are closed forms. These must be combated because they exclude not only human dialogue but also the intervention of the Word of God (264). Specifically, he objects to "administrative secrecy" and to structuralist ideology (266-67).

Ellul's specific ethical suggestions in this coda are highly provocative since they undoubtedly match our experiences of closed and incomprehensible language, the doublespeak of government administration, or any of the other destructions of language he mentions. These directives must be read against the backdrop of Ellul's recognition of false images as visible signs of invisible powers.[18] In our society iconoclasm is even more important than formerly, in that "all divine and demonic power is at stake, since its essence lies in these visible signs" (95). We should also note Ellul's various ethical exhortations in relation to the problem of propaganda[19] and the consequent need for Christians to think clearly about the way in which their language can express freedom in Christ rather than bondage to the powers. For example, suppose we wield truth in our congregations by forbidding any propagandizing or ideological language in our presbytery or district business meetings, by preaching open truth without hidden agendas in our sermons, by avoiding doublespeak in parish life, but instead conversing graciously and precisely and honestly.

My main point is that the Christian community is the place in which we practice "truthing" with each other, so that our language and work and politics and relationships throughout life flow out of the same character and thereby cast out the workings of the powers that produce deception, manipulation, accusation, and other untruths in the world. For example, in Chapter 3 we saw from two *Atlantic Monthly* articles how the ideological convictions about greenhouse gases and toxic pollution have prevented people, especially in the U.S., from entering into the weakness of our sisters and brothers in other places to know their genuine needs. Could the habit of speaking/living truth in our churches so equip the members of the Body to speak truth to powers in their daily occupations, such as journal-

18. See Jacques Ellul, *The New Demons*, trans. C. Edward Hopkin (New York: Seabury Press, 1975).

19. See Jacques Ellul, *Propaganda: The Formation of Men's Attitudes*, trans. Konrad Kellen and Jean Lerner (New York: Alfred A. Knopf, 1965).

ism, that Christians confound such presumption and stir up right awareness, as did William Langewiesche, Daniel Sarewitz, and Roger Pielke Jr.?
Wearing the belt of truth as an offensive weapon will call us all, individu-
ally and corporately, as Thomas More declares in Robert Bolt's play, *A Man
for All Seasons*, to "serve God wittily, in the tangle of our minds."[20]

It is crucial that we recognize the "tangle," for the "truthings" of our life
all hang together and influence each other, even as a small untruth leads to
much larger consequences. Ephesians 6 lists truth first because its absence
affects everything, but if the belt is used properly it can keep things together.

Jean Bethke Elshtain discusses the importance of rightly naming things
and cites James Q. Wilson, who recognized that we do not successfully
combat violent crime and deterioration in our cities if we decide that the
little things don't matter and let them slide. We must especially be truthful
about minor misdemeanors and petty sins

> because letting the little things go, ignoring the beginnings of deteri-
> oration and decrepitude, is a sign that we no longer care about this
> place; we do not mind if people start to trash it. This has an insidious
> effect on our hearts and minds. We are dragged down and some are
> drawn into the process of active destruction.[21]

Then Elshtain adds, "The deterioration, manipulation, and distortion of
language works in a similar fashion."[22] Caring about truth in every dimension of the Church's life and of Christians' lives is a necessary foundation
for the justice building, peacemaking, hospitality, and gospel proclaiming
that we will discuss as we continue to consider what it might mean for us
to wield God's panoply.

The Breastplate of Righteousness/Justice

Nicholas Wolterstorff shows how the breastplate of righteousness, which
begins in the weakness of accepting God's holiness and giving up on our

---

20. Quoted in Jean Bethke Elshtain, *Who Are We? Critical Reflections and Hopeful
Possibilities* (Grand Rapids: Wm. B. Eerdmans Publishing Co., 2000), p. 6.
21. Elshtain, *Who Are We?* p. 131.
22. Elshtain, *Who Are We?* p. 132.

own efforts to become righteous, becomes an offensive weapon that we as Church wield to challenge (especially economic) powers to their true vocation. He describes the call to Israel, which is also a call to the Christian Body as the branch grafted onto Israel, as follows:

> Holiness was not only set-apartness; holiness was also unity, purity, completeness, perfection. And the idea behind the Mosaic legislation seems to have been that Israel's being holy to God is as much task as status: Israel is to *become* holy and to *institute* into its life memorial remembrances of God's holiness. It is to become unified, pure, complete, and perfect like unto God's; and it is to incorporate quasiliturgical memorials of God's holiness in its life. In its life it is to imitate and celebrate the holiness of God. And for that, it must do justice. Injustice is a form of desecration. Justice is sacral. The call to justice is grounded in the call to be holy even as God is holy.[23]

Notice again the constant interplay of dimensions of being Church — participating in worship and fulfilling the way of life revealed in the character of the God we worship. Endowed with the panoply of God, we gird on the breastplate of righteousness as an offensive weapon that protects life-sustaining organs as we attack the walls of injustice, the munitions of oppression, the barricades of poverty, the barriers that thwart and break people.

Since there are countless ways in which churches build justice, let me focus on two for this chapter — the offering of hospitality and securing justice for victims. One of the best books published recently that shows the hospitality aspect of living justice from a weakness perspective is Christine Pohl's *Making Room*. She displays clearly the shocking nature of God's hospitality and our weakness within the power of God in this comment:

> God's guest list includes a disconcerting number of poor and broken people, those who appear to bring little to any gathering except their need. The distinctive quality of Christian hospitality is that it offers a generous welcome to the "least,"[24] without concern for advantage or

---

23. Nicholas Wolterstorff, "The Contours of Justice: An Ancient Call for Shalom," in Lampman and Shattuck, eds., *God and the Victim*, p. 121.

24. Matt. 26:40, 45. [Pohl's footnote.]

benefit to the host. Such hospitality reflects God's greater hospitality that welcomes the undeserving, provides the lonely with a home, and sets a banquet table for the hungry.[25]

Pohl demonstrates thoroughly that hospitality is not possible unless those who offer it are "also deeply aware of their own needs, frailties, and dependence on others" — what this book has been calling "weakness." After extensive interviews with practitioners, Pohl noted that many named a conversion of sorts as the starting point for their hospitality — a revision in their thinking when they perceived, "I'm not here because I'm helping them. I'm here because we're helping each other." One person, actively engaged in the "hard work of hospitality," had come to understand that "I myself am poor, that I myself am needy. That I walk the same pilgrimage that many of these people walk, just in a different format" (72).

Pohl recognizes that the weaknesses of guests and hosts are different. "Vulnerable strangers in need of welcome are usually marginal to the society because they are detached from significant human relationships and social institutions; often they are overlooked and undervalued by people more centrally situated." In contrast, hosts often consciously choose their marginality, and it is of a different sort: "it most often involves a certain distance rather than detachment from important social institutions. It may also involve a deliberate withdrawal from prevailing understandings of power, status, and possessions." Those who separate themselves from such powers "are often distinguished from the larger society by their practices, commitments, and distinctive ways of life" (105).

As we have seen under different terminology in Chapter 2, "The Bible makes the experience of marginality normative for the people of God." Pohl elaborates this biblical basis:

> For the Israelites and the early Christians, understanding themselves as aliens and sojourners was a reminder of their dependence on God. It provided a basis for gratitude and obedience. For the Israelites, especially, it was also connected to recognizing the feelings and vulnerabilities of the literal aliens who lived among them. Alien status for

25. Christine D. Pohl, *Making Room: Recovering Hospitality as a Christian Tradition* (Grand Rapids: Wm. B. Eerdmans Publishing Co., 1999), p. 16. Page references to this book in the following paragraphs will be given parenthetically in the text.

the early Christians suggested a basis for a different way of life and loyalties to a different order, which in turn challenged conventional boundaries and relationships. In emphasizing that both provision and welcome came as grace, the early Christians shared their lives and possessions with one another and transcended significant social and ethnic differences. Alien status allowed them to recognize the importance of making a home on earth and of nurturing the practice of hospitality, but it also relativized and transformed the experience of "home." While home was important, it was also provisional.

Jesus makes hospitality more complicated for Christians. We offer hospitality within the context of knowing Jesus as both our greater host and our potential guest. The grace we experience in receiving Jesus' welcome energizes our hospitality while it undermines our pride and self-righteousness. The possibility of welcoming Christ as our guest strengthens our kindness and fortitude in responding to strangers. . . .

The most transformative expressions of hospitality, both historically and in our own time, are associated with hosts who are liminal, marginal, or at the lower end of the social order. These hosts are essentially threshold or bridge people, connected in some ways to the larger society, but distinct from it either in actual social situation or in self-imposed distance. (105-6)

We have to keep in mind Pohl's phrase "the most transformative expressions of hospitality." Other kinds that operate out of their own power might produce more noticeable results — more admirable facilities or greater numbers of people served or whatever — but genuinely *shared* hospitality, which must correlatively come from weakness, will be more transformative.

In Chapter 3 we saw that churches which fall to the temptations of other powers then act as a fallen power themselves and violate their own vocation. On the other hand, let us notice throughout this chapter that when the Church fulfills its vocation as a power and lives, in this case, wielding the breastplate of righteousness, it will expose other powers and triumph over them.

Hospitality is an excellent example. Jean Vanier, French Canadian founder of the "L'Arche" communities, which now bring together volunteers from all over the world to live and work side by side with those called "handicapped," rejoices that the friendships and new "family" life in the households eliminate distinctions. The result is "a way of life absolutely opposed to the values of a competitive, hierarchical society in which the weak are pushed aside."[26]

Similarly, notice how many of our society's gods are displaced in this description from Pohl:

These hospitality communities embody a decidedly different set of values; their view of possessions and attitudes toward position and work differ from those of the larger culture. They explicitly distance themselves from contemporary emphases on efficiency, measurable results, and bureaucratic organization. Their lives together are intentionally less individualistic, materialistic, and task-driven than most in our society. In allying themselves with needy strangers, they come face-to-face with the limits of a "problem-solving" or a "success" orientation. In situations of severe disability, terminal illness, or overwhelming need, the problem cannot necessarily be "solved." But practitioners understand the crucial ministry of presence: it may not fix a problem but it provides relationships which open up a new kind of healing and hope. (112)

Against the gods elevated by the technicization of our culture, Pohl advocates these relationships, which become the locus for what in this book we have called "tabernacling." But as Pohl's book thoroughly displays, such hospitality is a lost art — and lost to a great extent because justice is often offered from a position of pride and power instead of weakness. Once again, human strength gets in the way of God's and demonstrates the importance of "power coming to an end," as we interpreted 2 Corinthians 12:9 in Chapter 2.

Pohl describes the sort of hospitality that "keeps people needy strangers while fostering an illusion of relationship and connection. It both disempowers and domesticates guests while it reinforces the hosts' power, control, and sense of generosity." Such false hospitality (note the interconnection of justice with the belt of truth) is "profoundly destructive to the people it welcomes." Only when the hosts "recognize their own need and inadequacy" — their weakness comparable to that of those to whom they minister — can "the power differential between hosts and guests" be di-

26. Jean Vanier, *The Heart of L'Arche: A Spirituality for Every Day* (New York: Crossroad, 1995), p. 29.

minished. Pohl concludes that "Humility is a crucial virtue for hospitality, and especially important in keeping hosts' power in check" (120).

The weakness that churches will experience in offering hospitality also arises because "We cannot separate the goodness and the beauty of hospitality from its difficulty. In a paradoxical way, hospitality is simultaneously mundane and sturdy, mysterious and fragile." The mundane chores include practical offerings such as making soup and bread or providing blankets and beds. But hospitality "always involves more than these, and certain tensions internal to hospitality make it fragile — vulnerable to distortion and misuse" (127).

Hospitality also requires boundaries — a necessary "concession to human finiteness" — but these are "never imposed without regret for the cost and loss involved" (129). Many years ago, Christians Equipped for Ministry, under which I freelance as a theologian, also sponsored the EPHESUS Community, in which I lived with a few other women, to provide temporary shelter and care for women coming out of drug/alcohol problems or away from abuse. To our deep distress, we once had to return a woman to the streets because her mental illness was threatening the life of the whole community. In our weakness, there was no alternative. It was painfully (and frighteningly) obvious that we didn't have the skills to deal with her situation. Eventually a "Bread and Roses" Catholic Worker house of hospitality took over the work entirely, but not before it stirred in me an unquenchable yearning to be more hospitable than my health and work limitations allow.

But that last sentence reveals a very important struggle. Is my work more important than hospitality, wholehearted caring for my neighbor?

Hospitality cannot be given merely by contributions to charities. It requires giving of myself — my time, my energy, my home, my friendship, my faith, my resources, my whole self. Should I take fewer speaking engagements or fewer writing assignments to have more time to offer genuine hospitality to those suffering injustice?

Our churches, too, must constantly wrestle. How can we, corporately, be more thoroughly hospitable to our neighbors? How can we be more supportive of the spiritual struggling of church members as each of our busy lives and our life together are challenged to make more space and time for others, remembering Jesus' affirmation that when our welcoming care is offered to them it is truly offered to himself?

Pohl helps us wrestle (in the examination of our personal and community lives) by beginning her book with a compelling set of questions setting out the concerns she will then explore. Among her questions are these, which raise the issues of power and weakness:

> Where does hospitality fit in the biblical story and in our identity as children of God? Why does Jesus, both as needy guest and gracious host, make hospitality compelling for us? What does the ancient church teach about a distinctive form of Christian hospitality? . . .
>
> If hospitality was so important in the ancient church, why and how did it get lost in later centuries? When hospitality was vibrant, where did it happen? What settings and social changes undermined hospitality as a personal and a church practice? What happened when concerns about hospitality led to specialized institutions separate from the church?
>
> What makes hospitality potentially subversive and countercultural? . . . Can some forms of hospitality humiliate persons in need? . . .
>
> Why is the experience of being a stranger crucial to being a good and gracious host? What is the relation between hospitality, seeing ourselves as aliens and sojourners, and our attitudes toward property and possessions? How are hospitality and power related?
>
> Why is hospitality so easily distorted — what makes it a fragile practice? Why does using hospitality instrumentally or for advantage undermine it? (14-15)

Perhaps our churches could ask these questions in a congregational discussion to discover what hospitality might mean for our particular communities. Does your parish agree that hospitality is a lost art? How might the specific weaknesses of your own church contribute to recovering the gifts of this practice?[27]

27. For other excellent resources to guide our thinking about being Church and doing justice, see also Craig L. Blomberg, *Neither Poverty nor Riches: A Biblical Theology of Material Possessions*, New Studies in Biblical Theology, series ed. D. A. Carson (Grand Rapids: Wm. B. Eerdmans Publishing Co., 1999); Rodney Clapp, ed., *The Consuming Passion: Christianity and the Consumer Culture* (Downers Grove, IL: InterVarsity Press, 1998); David P. Gushee, ed., *Toward a Just and Caring Society: Christian Responses to Poverty in America* (Grand Rapids: Baker Book House, 1999); and Ron Sider, *Just Generosity: A New Vision for Overcoming Poverty in America* (Grand Rapids: Baker Book House, 1999).

Another dimension that serves as an example of righteousness/justice that has been lost in our churches' move from positions of weakness to power is that of justice for victims. Howard Zehr quotes Julian Pleasants,[28] who chronicles the theological movement away from concern for the victim's *shalom* toward seeing crime as a violation of a higher authority (paralleling the same process in history for the political powers). Zehr concludes that

> In short, traditional Christianity has worked to release the offender from guilt while leaving the victim still hurting. In contrast, Pleasants notes, God's plan was to reinforce the importance of human victims by identifying with them: that is a core meaning of the cross. Referring to Andrew Wung Park's book entitled *The Asian Concept of Han and the Christian Concept of Sin,* Pleasants argues that God's heart is wounded by the hurt of the victim more than by the sinner's breaking of the law. In contrast, Western concepts of justice make law-breaking central to both justice and salvation.[29]

Zehr then calls for biblical justice, which works for the fullness of *shalom* for both perpetrator and victim.

Christian communities' efforts to *be with* crime victims as they work toward recovery, Mennonite efforts to build restitution programs into criminal incarceration programs, compassionate programs to care for the families of offenders, halfway houses that enable ex-offenders to move back into society with Christian mentoring, and efforts to prevent crime by providing tutoring, supervised play, and other possibilities for relationships for children prone to crime because of unjust environments — all these are efforts I have seen churches undertake. As Pohl has made clear, most effective are those that are offered in a spirit of companionable hospitality (that is, in weakness) rather than with pride-full hospitality (from our own strength), which, in Philip Hallie's words, "fills their hands but breaks their hearts."[30]

28. Julian Pleasants, "Religion that Restores Victims," *New Theology Review* 9, no. 3 (August 1996): 41-63.

29. Howard Zehr, "Restoring Justice," in Lampman and Shattuck, eds., *God and the Victim,* p. 141.

30. Philip Hallie, *Tales of Good and Evil, Help and Harm* (New York: HarperCollins, 1997), p. 207.

Shoes of Readiness to Proclaim the Gospel of Peace

It is significant that the weapon of shoes does not represent peace itself, but the readiness to proclaim it. This metaphor underscores the weakness dimension of this aspect of the Church's vocation because we proclaim, in all humility, what cannot yet be seen, and we work with confidence for what the world's powers cannot fathom — especially because we work for it not out of power or coercion, but in the way of Jesus whom we follow.

The Ephesians 6 metaphor of having put on shoes of readiness to proclaim the gospel of peace is a startling juxtaposition. In biblical times, of course, usually only soldiers would wear shoes, which were necessary to protect their feet in battle. Heralds, on the other hand, who ran with the *euangelion,* the good news of victory, wouldn't bother with heavy shoes in order to run swiftly for purposes of proclamation. The juxtaposition heightens our awareness that to proclaim *this* good news — of the genuine peace of the only true God — will engage us in confrontations with other powers.

Such confrontation was illustrated at the January 2000 meeting of the Society of Christian Ethics by a seminar discussion of the book *Just Peacemaking,* edited by Glen Stassen.[31] One of the chief objections to the writing team's work, leveled first by respondent Lisa Sowle Cahill, was that it is difficult to persuade those who will derive no benefit from them to engage in the practices of restraint and sacrifice that "just peacemaking" entails. For example, how can we induce rich citizens of the United States to limit their consumption of world resources so that better economic conditions can be developed in Two-Thirds World nations, where violence is often the result of entrenched injustice (and other workings of the fallen powers)?

Cahill's point is poignant: the wealthy are too enthralled by mammon to be willing to fight the results of their idolatry as that bears evil fruit in the violence of less affluent countries. The Church's work is to expose such idolatries, to form community members who resist the allures of possessions and instead practice restraint and sacrifice. The connection of the shoes of readiness with the breastplate of righteousness is essential.

31. Stassen, ed., *Just Peacemaking: Ten Practices for Abolishing War.* Let me stress that, despite the objection mentioned in the text above, this book contains excellent suggestions, resources, and encouragement for participation in God's work of peacemaking.

As Yoder Neufeld perceives from his study of the Divine Warrior imagery, "Unlike in Isaiah 59, when God could find no one to intervene, for the church to be wearing justice on its breast means that now there is someone to intervene." Now there is a people formed to be God's agent, to bring God's *shalom* in practical care — and this community is eager to be about God's work and word. "As valuable as is firm footwear, 'readiness' communicates the holy impatience to get the good news of peace out."[32]

We speak of what cannot yet be seen. However, the Christian community can speak this prophetic and stupendous word because of the coming *Parousia*. We are people of the future, Jacques Ellul exults in *The Presence of the Kingdom*, "not of a temporal and logical future, but of the *eschaton*, of the coming break with this present world." As a result, he claims, we look forward to the fulfillment, and all things "acquire their value in light of the coming Kingdom of God, in the light of the Judgment, and the victory of God."[33]

Christians live according to the reality, here and now, of the *eschaton*. The Christian life does not spring from a "cause," which often becomes an idolatry and often tempts us to abuse power. Instead, Christian life moves toward an "end," the goal of God's fulfillment of the kingdom,[34] which we receive both now and in the end by God's tabernacling in our weakness and at the end of time (2 Cor. 12:9-10 and Rev. 21:3).

Meanwhile, the Church not only lives in light of the future *shalom* of God and proclaims it to our neighbors; we also take steps together in humility to display the meaning of God's peace. By our practices in the congregation, we gain skills in reconciliation applicable to our other relationships outside of the community. May our life as a community of peace make ready an interest on the part of our neighbors in hearing the good news of God's *shalom*, which we proclaim in Christ.

Johann Christoph Arnold of the Bruderhof offers gentle suggestions and stories of practices to help us be a people living and proclaiming and making peace. After listing the paradoxes of seeking peace, including the "strength of weakness," Arnold presents chapters on stepping stones to peace, including "Simplicity, Silence, Surrender, Prayer, Trust, Forgiveness, Gratitude, Honesty, Humility, Obedience, Decisiveness, Repentance, Con-

---

32. Yoder Neufeld, *Ephesians*, manuscript p. 411.
33. Ellul, *Presence of the Kingdom*, p. 49.
34. Ellul, *Presence of the Kingdom*, pp. 49-52.

viction, Realism, and Service." It is obvious that these are not practices of power, but means by which we submit to God and to one another for the sake of receiving and displaying the *shalom* of God in our communities and toward the world. These steps, Arnold records, will result in "The Abundant Life" with its Security, Wholeness, Joy, Action, Justice, and Hope.[35]

I can't stress enough the crucial significance of the Church's paradigm of weakness as our "readiness" to proclaim the gospel of peace, nor can I emphasize sufficiently that this way of life runs counter to the world's (idolatrous) demand for instant gratification and "exciting" enjoyment. Since these virtues are essentially formed by a Christian community that embodies both the readiness and the alternativity of the gospel, we can learn them well from other members of the Body who are wise practitioners. Mark Harris's introduction to the work of Evelyn Underhill offers excellent training, as follows:

> Underhill counsels, "*Be* simple and dependent, acknowledge once for all the plain fact that you have nothing of your own, offer your life to God and trust Him with the ins and outs of your soul as well as everything else!" Living in the disciplined serenity of a posture of trust, Underhill invites us to something far richer than the most spectacular and dramatic of spiritual highs: "Keep the deep steady permanent peace, in the long run [it is] more precious and more fruitful than the dazzling light." Those who trust in God's grace take the long view. They have learned, with Underhill, that it is "the steady course, not the ecstasy, that counts in the end."[36]

It is indeed in the weakness of offering our lives to God in trust that Triune peace can be most authentically proclaimed.

---

35. Johann Christoph Arnold, *Seeking Peace: Notes and Conversations Along the Way* (Farmington, PA: The Plough Publishing House, 1998).

36. Mark Harris, *Companions for Your Spiritual Journey: Discovering the Disciplines of the Saints* (Downers Grove, IL: InterVarsity Press, 1999), p. 82, quoting *The Letters of Evelyn Underhill*, ed. Charles Williams (London: Longmans, Green, 1943), pp. 306, 312, and 311.

The Shield of Faith to Quench All the
Flaming Arrows of the Evil One

In the past I have thought about the shield of faith primarily as a defensive weapon, albeit a communal one, since each Roman soldier held his shield partly over the man next to him to create an interlocking wall of defense. It is essential to retain this communal orientation in discussing the shield, but we can also look more positively at how the Body of Christ wields faith.

As Tom Yoder Neufeld points out, this defensive wall of shields was necessary because the army would be attacking the enemy stronghold or walled city, from which the opponents might rain down the "fiery darts." Thus, when we apply the metaphor to the peaceful witness of the Church against the powers, the shield of faith signifies not only *trust* or *confidence* in God's power as a critical part of the armor, but also "putting on the shield is to participate in Messianic *faithfulness.*"[37]

A superb example of faithfulness as a positive (and often very surprising) gift that snuffs out evil was provided by Ken Butigan, author of a wonderful workbook/discussion guide on peacemaking,[38] at the World Trade Organization's conference in Seattle in November of 1999 (introduced in the first chapter). Ken, peacefully protesting against the global economy that causes many to suffer, found himself standing in front of the Nike store to protect its windows from smashers and looters. Certainly it was odd that peaceful protestors found themselves protecting a company that often received their criticisms, but they knew it was the right thing to do against the organized anarchists who intended to incite the crowd. Similarly, many of the protestors returned the next day and took up brooms to help clean up the damage done by the vandals.[39]

That kind of faithfulness — consistently opposing violence in all its forms — is God's method for building *shalom* in the world. It demon-

37. Yoder Neufeld, *Ephesians,* manuscript pp. 412-13.

38. See Ken Butigan, with Patricia Bruno, O.P., *From Violence to Wholeness* (Las Vegas, NV: Pace e Bene Franciscan Nonviolence Center, 1999). Additional study materials for using this "ten part program in the spirituality and practice of active nonviolence" can be obtained from the Lutheran Peace Fellowship, 1710 Eleventh Ave., Seattle, WA 98122; telephone (206) 720-0313; lpf@ecunet.org; www.nonviolence.org/lpf.

39. See Timothy Egan, "Black Masks Lead to Pointed Fingers in Seattle," *New York Times,* 2 December 1999, A1 and A14.

strates the weakness of compassion, for Butigan's action showed him moving not with power for the *cause* of opposition to child labor, but toward the *end* of faithful care for his neighbors, near and far.

Again we see the interrelatedness of the elements of God's armor — for faithfulness, especially in its communal support, undergirds the use of all the other weapons in the panoply. For example, in the need for the Church to wear the belt of truthful identity and proclaim the genuine wisdom of the gospel's peace in a culture of fragmentation and data overload, faithful integrity in a communitarian way of life that follows Jesus and takes up the cross is a vital component.

Hugh Mackay observes two major threats to Australian society (and I think also to North American society), which seem to be major arenas for the Church's display of faithfulness. He writes,

> [W]e are in danger of allowing our new-found acceptance of diversity and our embrace of the truly pluralistic society to rob us of a necessary sense of identity; a sense of where we came from and where we're going; a sense, above all, that we each have a safe place here — a place to call our own.
>
> Another major threat to our psychological and cultural health is coming from the information revolution, with its promise of that greatest of all modern hoaxes, the global village.
>
> How we deal with these two closely-related issues will determine the shape of Australian society over the next 25 years.[40]

Truly the Church offers its neighbors a genuine identity in the community of weakness that receives the tabernacling of God and also offers a gracious global community in Christ's Body, the Church, which stretches throughout time and space. Even Mackay recognizes that such community is the best weapon we have to counteract these threats, for he concludes his introduction with this recognition: "our most precious resource for coping with the inherently unstable and unpredictable world of the 21st century is not information, but each other."[41]

How essential it is that we keep remembering that it is the community

---

40. Hugh Mackay, *Turning Point: Australians Choosing Their Future* (Sydney: Pan Macmillan Australia, 1999), pp. xxxi-xxxii.

41. Mackay, *Turning Point*, p. xxxix.

which wears God's armor, that part of our weakness is our need for the whole Body to create God's new mode of being. As Jacques Ellul reminds us, "the first thing to do is to be faithful to revelation, but this fidelity can only become a reality in daily life through the creation of this new way of life: this is the 'missing link.'"[42] He goes on to emphasize the rebuilding of parish life, of discovering Christian community, "so that people may learn afresh what the fruit of the Spirit is (a very different thing from human 'virtues')."[43]

One crucial aspect of wielding faithfulness against the powers of our times, I believe, is the great sacrifice of caring for children, mentoring them, and raising them in the faith. At a discussion of my book *Is It a Lost Cause?* at the January 2000 meeting of the Society of Christian Ethics, members of the table group lamented how difficult it is to resist such powers as mammon (especially as propounded by television or "concerned" grandparents who might not understand our choices to live more simply in order to desacralize our culture's gods). Parents also particularly need support from other members in the Body to escape the lure of professional status, for example, the demand that parents spend so much time at work that little is left for their children, which can have a detrimental effect on their children's growth in faith and trust.[44] My discussion partners agreed on the urgent necessity for members of congregations to be more explicit in supporting each other's choice for weakness against the culture's powers for the sake of God's tabernacling in our children.[45]

The Roman army's interlocking shields made its attacking thrust virtu-

---

42. Ellul, *Presence of the Kingdom,* p. 145.

43. Ellul, *Presence of the Kingdom,* p. 150.

44. An important compendium of educational research, *Exploring Children's Spiritual Formation: Foundational Issues,* ed. Shirley K. Morgenthaler (River Forest, IL: Pillars Press, 1999), reports that children who have not been consistently held, responded to, and affirmed in their first eighteen months will have trouble with trust for the rest of their lives. They might gain cognitive skills, but in times of stress they will usually revert to their emotional experience of abandonment. See especially in that volume Stanley N. Graven, "Things that Matter in the Lives of Children: Looking at Children's Spiritual Development from a Developmentalist Perspective," pp. 39-68, and Shirley K. Morgenthaler, "Discussion," pp. 69-76.

45. For suggestions and discussion questions for study groups, see Marva J. Dawn, *Is It a Lost Cause? Having the Heart of God for the Church's Children* (Grand Rapids: Wm. B. Eerdmans Publishing Co., 1997).

ally invincible. Can we Christians learn such dependence on each other that our communities can become closely knit shields of mutual support to enable us to stand against the fiery darts of the powers that pull us away from faithfulness? Could churches, for example, more thoroughly share their financial resources to enable a parent or grandparent to stay home to care for the children and equip them with trust? Could we bolster each other's intentions to resist the seduction of professional status that demands time needed for our spiritual and family life?

The Helmet of Salvation/Liberation for Others

The metaphor of the helmet of salvation can easily be turned into a cozy capping of a believer's good fortune that she or he is protected from all evil by personal salvation — but that is to ignore both the wider biblical imagery of salvation as communal and cosmic and also the positive offensive use of the weapon. Tom Yoder Neufeld observes that "Within the context of putting on the armor, however, the image of grasping the helmet of salvation is meant to place on the church the task of bringing liberation to those in bondage by imitating the God of Isaiah 59." By means of his extensive dissertation studies on the biblical texts of the Divine Warrior, Yoder Neufeld shows how vocabulary supports this interpretation of Ephesians 6.[46]

How does the Church offer liberation to others out of its own weakness? I'm reminded of a humble pastor's response, when I asked how he managed to deal with a woman who suffered from great emotional and mental illnesses. "She wouldn't have any place at all if it weren't for the church," he said, "and I am patient with her to a fault." He remarked that he tries to be gentle but direct in delivering her from her illusions. Meanwhile, he lets her do what she can do as volunteer help. He realizes that she is able to help, but not well, so he simply tries to encourage her and pays the price of picking up the pieces afterward. What struck me most was the pastor's final comment: "I can't take all her hope away from her." The liberation wrought for her by this pastor's care and that of other congregation members creates a safe place for her to help diffuse her illusions, but also to keep her in hope — but it costs the community and especially the pastor extra time and effort.

46. Yoder Neufeld, *Ephesians*, manuscript p. 414.

Another and well-known example is provided by Magda Trocmé, who with her pastor husband André led the people of Le Chambon in France to rescue thousands of Jews during the Nazi occupation. When villagers were interviewed by Philip Hallie, they saw nothing extraordinary in what they did. They had simply lived out the liberation of Christ, as taught them by their pastor, in doing what was right for their neighbors. Philip Hallie was astonished to discover this amazing secret of the villagers and the Jews:

> Somewhere the American philosopher William James once wrote that habit is the flywheel of civilization; well, the habit of helping was the flywheel of the rescue machine of Le Chambon. Before I found Le Chambon I had thought of rescue — when I had thought of it at all — as the use of force to save somebody. I knew that for a long time, in the language of English and American law, rescue meant the forcible removal of somebody from legal custody. Not only in my own life, but in novels, in films, and in newspapers, strong-arm tactics have usually been the only means of rescuing somebody from harm. The hero or the cavalry arrives, and they save the victims by making the victimizers bite the dust. And so, though I was no stranger to compassionate help, I experienced one of the greatest shocks of my life when I realized that such an undramatic thing as the habit of helping was the living core of the rescue operation of Le Chambon.[47]

Hallie had searched and searched to find the secret that caused the villagers to risk their lives for so many strangers, but he kept finding the answer to be very simple: *"Toujours prête a servir,"* "Always ready to help." He remembered Magda Trocmé's greeting to new refugees, *"eh bien, naturellement, entrez, entrez."* He concludes, "And they came in, 'naturally,' 'of course,' and that was that."[48]

The Le Chambon case is particularly significant for our purposes here because the work of rescue required the entire village's cooperation. Liberation was accomplished by a *people* committed to daily acts of goodness in which God dwelt.

---

47. Hallie, *Tales of Good and Evil, Help and Harm,* p. 39.

48. Hallie, *Tales of Good and Evil, Help and Harm,* p. 37. See also Hallie's *Lest Innocent Blood Be Shed* (New York: Harper & Row, 1979, 1994).

Whatever liberation our churches bring to others must come not from our exertion of alternate (specifically oppressive) powers, but from the tabernacling of God in our particular community, guiding us to distinct ways to love our neighbors. Otherwise, we will end up as illustrations of what Jacques Ellul calls the "false presence of the kingdom." For example, it is not truly liberating if we participate in worthy (even biblical) causes just because the media make them the "issue of the day." Such fads and fashions pass away when they are no longer front-page news. Ellul instead urges us to continual prayer in order that we might discern what missions of liberation to undertake.[49] Only in the humility of weakness with regard to social pressures can we find God's true calling for our particular community.

Ellul emphasized more thoroughly in his original *Presence of the Kingdom* that God's liberating work can only be done through us if our churches are exhibiting God's character. He insists,

> The first truth which must be remembered, is that for Christians there is no dissociation between the end and the means . . . in the work of God the end and the means are identical. Thus when Jesus Christ is present the Kingdom has "come upon" us. This formula expresses very precisely the relation between the end and the means. Jesus Christ in his Incarnation appears as God's means, for the salvation of man and for the establishment of the Kingdom of God, but where Jesus Christ is, there also is this salvation and this kingdom.[50]

One of the elements of the Church's vocation, Ellul declares, is that we represent before the world this unity between end and means (80). I would add for our purposes here that one of the ways in which our churches defeat some powers and also restore others to their proper vocation is by demonstrating to the world this unity.

One of the keys to this is that the unity of end/means is paralleled by a unity in the community. Ellul adds that it cannot be thought of in individualistic terms, because we are thinking of *God* (81), and God's work of liberation is cosmic.

---

49. Ellul, *False Presence of the Kingdom,* pp. 85-86.

50. Ellul, *Presence of the Kingdom,* p. 79. Page references to this book in the following paragraphs will be given parenthetically in the text.

Ellul also won't let Christians settle for a cozy cap of salvation. He constantly describes the Christian life in terms of "the Holy Spirit, working within us, expressing himself in our actual life, through our words, our habits, and our decisions," so that the Christian "re-discovers his neighbour because he himself has been found by God" (95).

A superb example of this movement from personal salvation to wielding salvation for the sake of others is illustrated dramatically in John Grisham's gripping novel *The Testament*, which, as part of a quirky legal story, tells of a faithful character, the unknowing heiress of a mammoth fortune.[51]

I won't spoil the story by mentioning anything here about the legal problems, the lawyer Nate, his odyssey in handling the case, or his conversion. You need know for my purposes only that Nate himself experienced his own liberation — including one instance when the heiress miraculously appeared at the hospital and assured him that he wouldn't die, that God had sent her to protect him (367).

At the end of the book Nate

> stopped and turned for one last look at her hut. He wanted to take it with him, to lift it somehow and transport it to the States, to preserve it as a monument so that the millions of people she would touch could have a place to visit to say thanks. And her grave too. She deserved a shrine.
>
> That's the last thing she would want. (529)

Those yearnings in Nate arose because "Somehow she'd known he wasn't a drunk anymore, that his addictions were gone, that the demons who controlled his life had been forever locked away" (532). Instead she "had seen something good in him. Somehow she knew he was searching. She'd found his calling for him. God told her" (533).

In her will, Rachel Lane Porter had written this:

> The earnings from the trust are to be used for the following purposes: a) to continue the work of World Tribes missionaries around the world, b) to spread the Gospel of Christ, c) to protect the rights of indigenous people in Brazil and South America, d) to feed the hungry, heal the sick, shelter the homeless, save the children. (527)

51. John Grisham, *The Testament* (New York: Random House, 1999).

Would that all our churches had such a charter for passing on our own liberation!

The Sword of the Spirit, the Word of God

Most people have understood this metaphor to be the only offensive weapon of the panoply, so in keeping with the intentional paradoxical reversals of this book (meant to keep us mindful of the oddness, the countercultural twists, the alternativity of the Christian community's life) I would like to consider this aspect of the panoply not as a wielding of the Word in ethical pronouncements or proclamations of the gospel in preaching or teaching, but in the more subtle and almost passive sense of formation in and by the Word. Dorothy Day, co-founder with Peter Maurin of the Catholic Worker Movement, provides a superb model of one whose entire way of life and service (as well as that of the communities she developed) was characterized by the weakness of Jesus. In his biography of her, which reports on his extensive conversations with her, Robert Coles remarks that Dorothy often referred to the

> importance of "working from the bottom." Such would be the essential thrust of all Catholic Worker efforts: an intense, persisting localism, not as a step toward an eventual national effort, but itself the ultimate effort. This localism included both spiritual and political work. . . .
>
> This localism, she has observed, was "Christ's technique." She was always taking Jesus as seriously as possible; she was always trying to remember that He was an obscure carpenter who in His early thirties, did not go talk with emperors and kings and important officials, but with equally obscure people, and thereby persuaded a few fishermen, a few farm people, a few ailing and hard-pressed men and women, that there was reason for them to have great hope.[52]

Dorothy also had a biblically formed sense of time — and she lived in the knowledge of the *eschaton*, the fulfilling of God's purposes. This en-

---

52. Robert Coles, *Dorothy Day: A Radical Devotion*, Radcliffe Biography Series (Reading, MA: Addison-Wesley Publishing Co./Perseus Books, 1987), p. 90. Page references to this book in the following paragraphs will be given parenthetically in the text.

abled her to resist the methods of such powers as government and mammon for the sake of doing ministry in God's humble ways. An example might be when the Catholic Worker community was trying to unionize Ford factories or close them down and she would say, "The Lord hasn't closed them down yet, but what's a decade or two in His time? Sometimes when people call me a 'utopian,' I say, no, I just have a different sense of time than many others have." Coles continues,

> She realized full well that federal programs seemed to provide the answer to urgent problems, that in a relatively quick span of time a large sum of money can be appropriated to address a problem that seems, otherwise, intractable. She knew the power of the modern nation-state, its capacity to pull people together, its capacity to launch programs, to mobilize unparalleled resources. Her purposes were different, however, her approach directed at people's attitudes, at their moral lives, at their overall ethical purpose as human beings. She wanted to affect not just the overall problem, but people's everyday lives — their manner of living with one another. (96)

When young people who had come to work with the Movement commented, "You people are impractical, . . . nice idealists, but not headed anywhere big and important," she responded,

> They are right. We *are* impractical, as one of us put it, as impractical as Calvary. . . .
> We are here to bear witness to our Lord. We are here to follow His lead. We are here to celebrate Him through these works of mercy. We are here, I repeat, to follow His lead — to oppose war and the murder of our fellow human beings, to reach out to all we see and meet. We are *not* here to prove that our technique of working with the poor is useful, or to prove that we are able to be effective humanitarians. (97)

Dorothy Day understood profoundly two of the main themes that stirred me to write this book — that biblically formed faith is to be lived out in weakness and, as much as possible, that it is to be lived out as a community. She wielded the sword of the Spirit, the Word of God, in a politics that she described animatedly as a matter of "pursuing a community life, a community life which would be loyal to the teaching in the Sermon on the Mount." As Coles summarizes, she thought

> that if more and more such communities were to form, a local poli-
> tics would be at work and would affect the quality of more and more
> lives, and, she prayed, the nation as a whole. True, she was dreaming;
> she well knew that the communities she spoke of so fondly were a
> mere handful. Nevertheless, entire empires had been toppled by a
> handful of dissenters, men and women who seem to have no influ-
> ence and power and no interest in obtaining them. What they have
> done, she reminded me, is bear witness, stand fast, huddle together in
> faith, in community: the early followers of Jesus, for example.

Coles reports that for Dorothy Day, "just yesterday was when Jesus walked Galilee, and not far away will be the moment He decides to call us all to Him." He confesses that he did not rightly understand what she meant by that and that Dorothy had corrected him with this explanation:

> We are communities in time and in a place, I know, but we are com-
> munities in faith as well — and sometimes time can stop shadowing
> us. Our lives are touched by those who lived centuries ago, and we
> hope that our lives will mean something to people who won't be alive
> until centuries from now. It's a great "chain of being," someone once
> told me, and I think our job is to do the best we can to hold up our
> small segment of the chain. That's one kind of localism, I guess, and
> one kind of politics — doing your utmost to keep that chain con-
> nected, unbroken. Our arms are linked — we try to be neighbors of
> His, and to speak up for his principles. That's a lifetime's job. (109)

I have quoted this biography of Dorothy Day at such length because she so well exemplifies the theme of this book: resisting and overcoming the fallen powers not by acting as one, but by being the Church in weak-ness, so that Christ's power may tabernacle in us and the purposes of God might be fulfilled through us. When Robert Coles asked her how she would want to be described, she

> took up the challenge and repeated what I had heard before — her
> wish to be defined and remembered as a member of a particular

Christian community, as an ardent seeker after God who, with some devotion, had followed His example "after a few false starts." Then, after pausing to look out the window, after a retreat into silence, she said slowly, quoting the archbishop of Paris, Cardinal Suhard, "To be a witness does not consist in engaging in propaganda or even in stirring people up, but in being a living mystery; it means to live in such a way that one's life would not make sense if God did not exist." (159-60)

To that end may all our churches be so biblically formed as Dorothy Day and her Catholic Worker communities; and to become so, may we all wield the next piece of the panoply, the weapon of prayer!

Prayer at All Times, for All, in All Kinds, with All Perseverance

Prayer is the only element appearing both in the vision of Acts 2 (discussed in Chapter 3) and in the panoply of Ephesians 6, and that double appearance is significant for our purposes here, for, indeed, prayer is a critical means for understanding, disarming, resisting, and conquering the powers.[53] First of all, however, prayer must be wielded to purge from us our methods of power so that we can be weak for tabernacling. Great prayer saint Andrew Murray (1828-1917) exults,

> What a solemn, precious lesson! It is not to sin only that the cleansing of the Husbandman refers [John 15:1-3]. It is to our own religious activity, as it is developed in the very act of bearing fruit. In working for God our natural gifts of wisdom, or eloquence, or influence, or zeal are ever in danger of being unduly developed, and then trusted in. So, after each season of work, God has to bring us to the end of ourselves, to the consciousness of the helplessness and the danger of all that is of man, to feel that we are nothing. All that is to be left of us is just enough to receive the power of the life-giving sap of the Holy Spirit.

53. See Jacques Ellul, "Prayer as Combat," *Prayer and Modern Man,* trans. C. Edward Hopkin (New York: Seabury Press, 1970), pp. 139-78. For a discussion of prayer as a critical element of church life see Carnegie Samuel Calian, *Survival or Revival: Ten Keys to Church Vitality* (Louisville: Westminster John Knox Press, 1998).

What is of man must be reduced to its very lowest measure. All that is inconsistent with the most entire devotion to Christ's service must be removed. The more perfect the cleansing and cutting away of all that is of self, the less of surface over which the Holy Spirit is to be spread, so much the more intense can be the concentration of our whole being, to be entirely at the disposal of the Spirit.[54]

Such a warning is essential for us especially in this chapter since we have considered the panoply of God as offensive weapons wielded by churches against other powers and their dominions. Prayer constantly reminds us that even though we are actively engaged in the battle by means of this panoply, yet God is the Divine Warrior and we are weak for the sake of Triune power.

As with all the other elements of the armor and of being Church (in Chapter 3), prayer is too enormous a topic to be discussed thoroughly. My concern is simply that we pause a moment to consider the integral and inextricable connection of prayer and weakness with our churches' fulfilling of their true vocations as created powers in battle with fallen powers.

Donald E. Miller, the Episcopalian who wrote *The Case for Liberal Christianity* in the early 1980s and *Reinventing American Protestantism* in 1997, points out that more established mainline Christian communities have much to learn from the self-named "new paradigm churches."[55] Particularly for our purposes here, these churches offer vivid examples of wielding prayer for the sake of gospel witness.

Miller notes first that the movements are led by people with "immodest vision," that they are not limited by their own capacities and resources. In my terminology here, their weaknesses are available for God's purposes. Second, Miller observes, their

visions are typically not the result of megalomania, although the human element can never be fully removed. Rather, these dreams have

---

54. Andrew Murray, from *Day by Day,* quoted in *For All the Saints: A Prayer Book for and by the Church,* vol. 1: Year 1, Advent to the Day of Pentecost, compiled and edited by Frederick J. Schumacher with Dorothy A. Zelenko (Delhi, NY: American Lutheran Publicity Bureau, 1994), pp. 180-81.

55. Donald E. Miller, "The Reinvented Church: Styles and Strategies," *Christian Century* 116, no. 36 (22-29 December 1999): 1250-53.

come, quite literally, during periods of extended prayer and fasting. People have seen visions of what God is going to do in their city. Sometimes God even speaks audibly to them. In short, the very visitations that are described in the Hebrew scriptures and the New Testament seem still to be happening.[56]

As Miller declares, there are many other lessons to be learned from these churches, but the critical motif for us is this: prayer is the root of all our faithfulness. In the weakness of prayer, God visits — and stays.

In his foundational vision for *The Presence of the Kingdom* more than fifty years ago, Jacques Ellul had made the same point, that the Church's ministry starts in prayer. In the final two paragraphs of his 1948 call for the Church to display God's presence, he urges churches to resist cultural solutions and challenges them instead to find the way of God so that they can be "present in the world with the effectiveness given by the Holy Spirit."[57]

The fact that Ellul's call to weakness (though he didn't use that terminology) needs constantly to be reiterated heightens our awareness of what following Christ's way against the powers requires. Yet weakness is also the only way in which God can tabernacle and the powers can be conquered. This is why prayer is so crucial for the community:

The enemies of the Church seek to turn it aside from its own way, in order to make it follow their way; the moment it yields it becomes the play-thing of the forces of the world. It is given up to its adversaries. It can only have recourse to God in prayer, that He may teach it His way, which no one else can teach it. This means not only the way of eternal salvation, but the way which one follows in the land of the living, the way which is truly impossible to find unless God reveals it, truly impossible to follow with our human power alone. The problem is the same in the social and the individual sphere. From the human point of view this way of the Church in the world is foolish, Utopian, and ineffective, and we are seized with discouragement when we see what we really have to do in this real world. We might throw the whole thing up, were we not sure of seeing the goodness of the Lord in the land of the living: but we have seen this goodness, it

56. Miller, "The Reinvented Church," p. 1252.
57. Ellul, *Presence of the Kingdom,* p. 152.

has been manifested, and on this foundation we can go forward and confront the powers of this world, in spite of our impotence, for "in all these things we are more than conquerors through Him that loved us. For I am persuaded that neither death nor life, nor angels nor principalities, nor things present, nor things to come, nor powers, nor height nor depth, nor any other creature, shall be able to separate us from the love of God which is in Christ Jesus our Lord." Rom. 8.37-39.[58]

One of the participants at the Schaff Lectures gave me a superb example of congregational prayer, which shows how this element of the panoply brings together truthfulness, justice, fellowship and communal support, liberation and being formed by the Word of God. As a guest at a major inner-city church, he had witnessed a remarkable presentation of what I call "Churchbeing." During the congregational prayer/altar call, a young woman with tattered clothes and holding a tiny baby came forward. The pastor began looking around the large congregation and calling out names. In response, several women came forward from the crowd, and the pastor said to the young woman, "These are your new friends. They will support you, pray with you, help you in your new Christian life." Meanwhile, a young teen had also come forward, and the pastor similarly called out youth from the assembly. This entire congregation, it seems, is prepared to welcome strangers with the hospitality of true friendship, constant prayer, practical and liberating help and justice. Oh, that all our churches could be such a genuine community, that we could all be so immersed in, and transformed by, the Word and prayer!

Please Don't Let This Book End
When You Finish Reading

In the last section of Chapter 3 I quoted Hugh Mackay's assertion that the present time in Australia could be considered "ripe for a revival of religious faith and practice," but that the signs weren't pointing in that direction. He reiterated the same point on the last page of his book, observing that "Times of uncertainty — especially when linked with a half-formed

---

58. Ellul, *Presence of the Kingdom*, pp. 152-53.

sense of expectancy — have, in the past, been fertile breeding grounds for religious revivals," but more strongly he insisted that this "seems unlikely in our case."[59]

I found myself saying frequently to the groups for whom I was teaching "down under," "Will we let Mackay be right, or can our very weakness be the means for God to work here in new ways?" Could the same be true in North America, Europe, throughout the jaundiced West? Could the very opprobrium attached to Christianity by some media, could the very absence of religious experience in young adults who grew up in *Life After God* times, could the very rejection of the institutional church in our society also be vehicles of weakness for God's purposes to be accomplished?

I believe this could be a time of revival if we let weakness be the agent for God's tabernacling. I believe this strongly because of such hints as this closing comment from the narrator in Douglas Coupland's *Life After God*:

> Now — here is my secret:
> I tell it to you with an openness of heart that I doubt I shall ever achieve again, so I pray that you are in a quiet room as you hear these words. My secret is that I need God — that I am sick and can no longer make it alone. I need God to help me give, because I no longer seem to be capable of giving; to help me be kind, as I no longer seem capable of kindness; to help me love, as I seem beyond being able to love.[60]

Such longing stirs up my yearning for the Christian community to recover skills of hospitality and fellowship and liberation, for ministry out of our weakness and incapabilities to those who need God as we do.

We need not feel overwhelmed by the cultural forces arrayed against Christianity; the battle against the powers has already been decided. And we need not feel overwhelmed when we remember that such ending of our power as we might be feeling is exactly what Christ desires for the fullness of his tabernacling. As Jacques Ellul concludes, in the penultimate chapter on "Dominions and Powers" in *The Subversion of Christianity*,

---

59. Mackay, *Turning Point*, p. 302.

60. Douglas Coupland, *Life After God* (New York: Simon and Schuster, 1994), p. 359.

> The Holy Spirit gives hope where all is despair, the strength to endure in the midst of disaster, perspicacity not to fall victim to seduction, the ability to subvert in turn all the powers that are involved. Believers, then, are those who have the wisdom and strength to rob material realities of their seductive power, to unmask them for what they are, no more, and to put them in the service of God, diverting them totally from their own law.[61]

Ellul acknowledges that there is never any "imperial triumph" in human terms and times. The powers use the very gifts of God "to advance their own grandeur." We will never be done with this struggle, this cosmic battle, until the end of time.

But then Ellul begins his final chapter with this ringing proclamation:

> Nevertheless, Christ is there. The cross that is planted at the heart of the history of the world cannot be uprooted. The risen Christ is with us to the end of the world. The Holy Spirit acts in secret and with infinite patience. There is a church that is constantly born and reborn.[62]

The cross is the heart of history. In the name and tabernacling of the risen Christ, let us make it our churches' heart, too.

---

61. Jacques Ellul, *The Subversion of Christianity,* trans. Geoffrey W. Bromiley (Grand Rapids: Wm. B. Eerdmans Publishing Co., 1986), p. 190.
62. Ellul, *Subversion of Christianity,* p. 191.

Questions for Reflection
and Communal Conversation

I pray that this study leaves you with a yearning for your congregation to be reborn in weakness. Perhaps discussion of the following questions can contribute to renewal. You will recognize some of these questions from their earlier appearance in this book.

Chapter 1

1. How much and in what ways is my life and the life of the congregation in which I participate controlled by powers inimical to the gospel?
2. What aspects of these powers can be resisted, changed, overcome?
3. Which need to be ignored or avoided?
4. How can our church work together as a community in opposition to these powers?
5. Am I willing to do what it takes to stand against the powers invading our churches? Am I *really*?

Chapter 2

1. Why am I so afraid of weakness? Why do I struggle so much to operate out of power instead?
2. Are we in our weakness truly being the locus of God's tabernacling?
3. If the images and exhortations and stories of weakness are so pervasive

in the Scriptures, why is my church so rich? so strong? so popular? Or is it poor, weak, or marginal for the wrong reasons?

4. How could our congregation learn more deeply the hidden cruciform way of Jesus?

5. Why is this hiddenness of God in the utter humility of Christ so ardently rejected in our times?

Chapter 3

1. Is the sporting urge prevailing in our churches over the spiritual impulse?

2. What happens to church leaders who act out of their power or out of the pressures of power rather than out of the weakness that receives God's tabernacling?

3. Are our churches' goals set by slogans of the culture around us or by biblical texts? Do our congregational programs find their source in the way sociology defines the present "needs"/"wants" of consumers or in the Scriptures?

4. In what ways is my Christian community living as the early Christians of Acts 2 did?

5. What specific powers tempt our particular congregation away from its true vocation?

6. Which dimensions of our congregational life exhibit our church's fallenness? How could a theology of weakness restore those dimensions to their proper functioning under God's power?

7. Is my congregation acting as an agent of healings? Does my church notice the signs of God's mysterious interventions? Do we observe and praise the power of God at work through us?

8. Is revival not happening in our churches because we haven't become open enough to see God's signs and wonders, weak enough for God to move in with power?

9. Could our churches partner with inner-city churches to share financial and other resources? But if we do so, can we who are rich know our weakness enough to receive the immense gifts of our poorer brothers and sisters? Can our churches invite members to desacralize money in their own lives to work for global economic redistribution? Can we issue prophetic challenges to our members involved in multinational corporations to cease practices that exploit citizens of poorer nations?

How might our church budget be radically realigned for the sake of exposing mammon, disarming it, and triumphing over it in our corporate congregational life and in the personal lives of members?

Chapter 4

1. Why is the experience of being a stranger crucial to being a good and gracious host? What is the relation between hospitality, seeing ourselves as aliens and sojourners, and our attitudes toward property and possessions? How are hospitality and power related?
2. What weapons of the panoply does my congregation especially need to recover more thoroughly for more faithful following?
3. In what dimensions of our congregational life are we already battling the powers? How? What's happening in the struggle?
4. How could we as a congregation in this time and place learn more truly to Be Church? How could I, as part of the community?
5. How can I be God's agent in calling my community to the weakness in which God tabernacles?

Works Cited

Adams, James Luther. "We Wrestle Against Principalities and Powers." In *The Prophethood of All Believers*, ed. George K. Beach, pp. 165-72. Boston: Beacon Press, 1986.

Arnold, Johann Christoph. *Seeking Peace: Notes and Conversations Along the Way*. Farmington, PA: The Plough Publishing House, 1998.

Bailey, Kenneth E. *Poet and Peasant* and *Through Peasant Eyes: A Literary-Cultural Approach to the Parables in Luke*. Grand Rapids: Wm. B. Eerdmans Publishing Co., 1983.

Barnett, Paul. *The Second Epistle to the Corinthians*. Grand Rapids: Wm. B. Eerdmans Publishing Co., 1997.

Barrett, C. K. *A Commentary on the Second Epistle to the Corinthians*. New York: Harper and Row, Publishers, 1973.

―――. *The First Epistle to the Corinthians*. London: Adam and Charles Black, 1968.

Barth, Karl. *Church and State*. Trans. G. Ronald Howe. London: Student Christian Movement Press, 1939.

―――. *Church Dogmatics* IV, *The Christian Life*. Trans. Geoffrey W. Bromiley. Grand Rapids: Wm. B. Eerdmans Publishing Co., 1981.

―――. *Church Dogmatics* IV/2, *The Doctrine of Reconciliation*. Trans. Geoffrey W. Bromiley. Edinburgh: T. & T. Clark, 1958.

Barth, Markus. *The Broken Wall: A Study of the Epistle to the Ephesians*. Valley Forge, PA: Judson Press, 1959.

―――. *Ephesians: Introduction, Translation, and Commentary on Chapters 1–3*. Volume 34, part 1, of The Anchor Bible. William Foxwell Albright and David Noel Freedman, general editors. Garden City, NY: Doubleday and Company, 1974.

―――. *Ephesians: Translation and Commentary on Chapters 4–6*. Volume 34, part

2 of The Anchor Bible. William Foxwell Albright and David Noel Freedman, general editors. Garden City, NY: Doubleday and Company, 1974.

Berkhof, Hendrik. *Christ and the Powers.* Trans. John H. Yoder. Scottdale, PA: Herald Press, 1962.

Bernanos, Georges. *The Diary of a Country Priest.* Trans. Pamela Morris. Garden City, NY: Doubleday and Company, (1937), 1954.

——. *The Heroic Face of Innocence: Three Stories by Georges Bernanos.* Grand Rapids: Wm. B. Eerdmans Publishing Co., 1999.

Best, Ernest. *Second Corinthians: A Bible Commentary for Teaching and Preaching.* Interpretation Series. Louisville: John Knox Press, 1987.

Blomberg, Craig L. *Neither Poverty nor Riches: A Biblical Theology of Material Possessions.* New Studies in Biblical Theology. D. A. Carson, series editor. Grand Rapids: Wm. B. Eerdmans Publishing Co., 1999.

Bornkamm, Heinrich. *Luther's Doctrine of the Two Kingdoms: In the Context of His Theology.* Trans. Karl H. Hertz. Philadelphia: Fortress Press, 1966.

Bowen, Bob. "Driving Out the Demons." *Gospel Herald* 78, no. 20 (14 May 1985): 337.

Brown, Dale W. *Biblical Pacifism: A Peace Church Perspective.* Elgin, IL: Brethren Press, 1986.

Bruce, F. F. *1 and 2 Corinthians.* New Century Bible. London: Oliphants, 1971.

——. "Colossian Problems Part 4: Christ as Conqueror and Reconciler." *Bibliotheca Sacra* 141, no. 4 (Oct.-Dec. 1984): 291-302.

Bultmann, Rudolf. *Theology of the New Testament.* Volume 1. Trans. Kendrick Grobel. New York: Charles Scribner's Sons, 1951.

Butigan, Ken, with Patricia Bruno, O.P. *From Violence to Wholeness.* Las Vegas, NV: Pace e Bene Franciscan Nonviolence Center, 1999.

Caird, G. B. *Principalities and Powers: A Study in Pauline Theology.* Oxford: Clarendon Press, 1956.

Calian, Carnegie Samuel. *Survival or Revival: Ten Keys to Church Vitality.* Louisville: Westminster John Knox Press, 1998.

Cannon, George E. *The Use of Traditional Materials in Colossians.* Macon, GA: Mercer University Press, 1983.

Carr, Wesley. *Angels and Principalities: The Background, Meaning, and Development of the Pauline Phrase hai archai kai hai exousiai.* Cambridge: Cambridge University Press, 1981.

——. "The Rulers of This Age — I Corinthians II.6-8." *New Testament Studies* 23 (1976): 20-35.

Clapp, Rodney. *A Peculiar People: The Church as Culture in a Post-Christian Society.* Downers Grove, IL: InterVarsity Press, 1996.

Clapp, Rodney, ed. *The Consuming Passion: Christianity and the Consumer Culture.* Downers Grove, IL: InterVarsity Press, 1998.

Clarke, Erskine, ed. *Exilic Preaching: Testimony for Christian Exiles in an Increasingly Hostile Culture.* Harrisburg, PA: Trinity Press International, 1998.

Cobble, James F., Jr. *The Church and the Powers: A Theology of Church Structure.* Peabody, MA: Hendrickson Publishers, 1990.

Cochrane, Arthur C. *The Mystery of Peace.* Elgin, IL: Brethren Press, 1986.

Coles, Robert. *Dorothy Day: A Radical Devotion.* Radcliffe Biography Series. Reading, MA: Addison-Wesley Publishing Co./Perseus Books, 1987.

Coupland, Douglas. *Life After God.* New York: Simon and Schuster, 1994.

Cullmann, Oscar. *Christ and Time: The Primitive Christian Conception of Time and History.* Trans. Floyd V. Filson. Philadelphia: Westminster Press, 1950.

Danker, Frederick W. *II Corinthians.* Augsburg Commentary on the New Testament. Minneapolis: Augsburg Publishing House, 1989.

Dawn, Marva J. "The Concept of 'The Principalities and Powers' in the Works of Jacques Ellul." Ph.D. dissertation, The University of Notre Dame, 1992 (Ann Arbor, MI: University Microfilms, #9220014).

————. *I'm Lonely, LORD — How Long? Meditations on the Psalms.* Revised edition. Grand Rapids: Wm. B. Eerdmans Publishing Co., 1998.

————. *Is It a Lost Cause? Having the Heart of God for the Church's Children.* Grand Rapids: Wm. B. Eerdmans Publishing Co., 1997.

————. *Joy in Our Weakness: A Gift of Hope from the Book of Revelation.* St. Louis: Concordia Publishing House, 1994.

————. *Keeping the Sabbath Wholly: Ceasing, Resting, Embracing, Feasting.* Grand Rapids: Wm. B. Eerdmans Publishing Co., 1989.

————. *Reaching Out without Dumbing Down: A Theology of Worship for the Turn-of-the-Century Culture.* Grand Rapids: Wm. B. Eerdmans Publishing Co., 1995.

————. *A Royal "Waste" of Time: The Splendor of Worshiping God and Being Church for the World.* Grand Rapids: Wm. B. Eerdmans Publishing Co., 1999.

————. *To Walk and Not Faint: A Month of Meditations on Isaiah 40.* Revised edition. Grand Rapids: Wm. B. Eerdmans Publishing Co., 1997.

————. *Truly the Community: Romans 12 and How to Be the Church.* Grand Rapids: Wm. B. Eerdmans Publishing Co., 1992.

Dawn, Marva J., and Eugene Peterson. *The Unnecessary Pastor: Rediscovering the Call.* Grand Rapids: Wm. B. Eerdmans Publishing Co., 1999.

Dean, Kenda Creasy, ed. *Growing Up Postmodern: Imitating Christ in the Age of "Whatever."* Princeton, NJ: Institute for Youth Ministry, 1999.

de Caussade, Jean-Pierre. *The Sacrament of the Present Moment.* Trans. Kitty Muggeridge. San Francisco: Harper & Row, Publishers, 1982.

Earl, Lee A. "The Spiritual Problem of Crime: A Pastor's Call." In *God and the Victim: Theological Reflections on Evil, Victimization, Justice, and Forgiveness,* ed.

Lisa Barnes Lampman and Michelle Shattuck, pp. 235-49. Grand Rapids: Wm. B. Eerdmans Publishing Co., 1999.

Ellul, Jacques. *The Ethics of Freedom*. Trans. Geoffrey W. Bromiley. Grand Rapids: Wm. B. Eerdmans Publishing Co., 1976.

————. *False Presence of the Kingdom*. Trans. C. Edward Hopkin. New York: Seabury Press, 1972.

————. *The Humiliation of the Word*. Trans. Joyce Main Hanks. Grand Rapids: Wm. B. Eerdmans Publishing Co., 1985.

————. *Money and Power*. Trans. LaVonne Neff. Downers Grove, IL: InterVarsity Press, 1984.

————. *The New Demons*. Trans. C. Edward Hopkin. New York: Seabury Press, 1975.

————. *The Political Illusion*. Trans. Konrad Kellen. New York: Alfred A. Knopf, 1967.

————. *Prayer and Modern Man*. Trans. C. Edward Hopkin. New York: Seabury Press, 1970.

————. *The Presence of the Kingdom*. Trans. Olive Wyon. New York: Seabury Press, 1967.

————. *Propaganda: The Formation of Men's Attitudes*. Trans. Konrad Kellen and Jean Lerner. New York: Alfred A. Knopf, 1965.

————. *Sources and Trajectories: Eight Early Articles by Jacques Ellul That Set the Stage*. Trans. and ed. Marva J. Dawn. Grand Rapids: Wm. B. Eerdmans Publishing Co., 1997.

————. *The Subversion of Christianity*. Trans. Geoffrey W. Bromiley. Grand Rapids: Wm. B. Eerdmans Publishing Co., 1986.

————. *The Technological Bluff*. Trans. Joyce Main Hanks. Grand Rapids: Wm. B. Eerdmans Publishing Co., 1990.

————. *The Technological Society*. Trans. John Wilkinson. New York: Vintage Books, 1964.

————. *The Technological System*. Trans. Joachim Neugroschel. New York: Continuum Publishing Co., 1980.

————. *Violence: Reflections from a Christian Perspective*. Trans. Cecelia Gaul Kings. New York: Seabury Press, 1969.

Elshtain, Jean Bethke. *Who Are We? Critical Reflections and Hopeful Possibilities*. Grand Rapids: Wm. B. Eerdmans Publishing Co., 2000.

Erler, Rolf Joachim, and Reiner Marquard, eds. *A Karl Barth Reader*. Trans. and ed. Geoffrey W. Bromiley. Grand Rapids: Wm. B. Eerdmans Publishing Co., 1986.

Farley, Edward. *Deep Symbols: Their Postmodern Effacement and Reclamation*. Valley Forge, PA: Trinity Press International, 1996.

Farrow, Douglas. *Ascension and Ecclesia: On the Significance of the Doctrine of the*

Ascension for Ecclesiology and Christian Cosmology. Grand Rapids: Wm. B. Eerdmans Publishing Co., 2000.

Foster, Richard J. *The Challenge of the Disciplined Life: Christian Reflection on Money, Sex and Power*. San Francisco: Harper & Row, 1989.

Friesen, Duane K., John Langan, S.J., and Glen Stassen. "Introduction: Just Peacemaking as a New Ethic." In *Just Peacemaking: Ten Practices for Abolishing War*. Ed. Glen Stassen. Cleveland: Pilgrim Press, 1998.

Furnish, Victor Paul. *II Corinthians: Translated, with Introduction, Notes, and Commentary*. The Anchor Bible. Garden City, NY: Doubleday, 1984.

Gaventa, Beverly R. "He Comes as One Unknown." *Christian Century* 110, no. 36 (15 Dec. 1993): 1270-80.

Girard, René. *The Scapegoat*. Trans. Yvonne Freccero. Baltimore: Johns Hopkins University Press, 1986.

————. *Things Hidden Since the Foundation of the World*. Trans. Stephen Bann and Michael Metteer. Stanford: Stanford University Press, 1987.

————. *Violence and the Sacred*. Trans. Patrick Gregory. Baltimore: Johns Hopkins University Press, 1977.

Graven, Stanley N. "Things that Matter in the Lives of Children: Looking at Children's Spiritual Development from a Developmentalist Perspective." In *Exploring Children's Spiritual Formation: Foundational Issues*, ed. Shirley Morgenthaler, pp. 39-68. River Forest, IL: Pillars Press, 1999.

Grisham, John. *The Testament*. New York: Random House, 1999.

Guder, Darrell L. *The Continuing Conversion of the Church*. The Gospel and Our Culture Series. Craig Van Gelder, gen. ed. Grand Rapids: Wm. B. Eerdmans Publishing Co., 2000.

Gushee, David P., ed. *Toward a Just and Caring Society: Christian Responses to Poverty in America*. Grand Rapids: Baker Book House, 1999.

Hallie, Philip. *Lest Innocent Blood Be Shed*. New York: Harper & Row, 1979, 1994.

————. *Tales of Good and Evil, Help and Harm*. New York: Harper-Collins, 1997.

Harris, Mark. *Companions for Your Spiritual Journey: Discovering the Disciplines of the Saints*. Downers Grove, IL: InterVarsity Press, 1999.

Holloway, James Y., ed. *Introducing Jacques Ellul*. Grand Rapids: Wm. B. Eerdmans Publishing Co., 1970.

Hughes, Philip Edgcumbe. *Paul's Second Epistle to the Corinthians*. Grand Rapids: Wm. B. Eerdmans Publishing Co., 1971.

The Hutterian Society of Brothers and John Howard Yoder, eds. *God's Revolution: The Witness of Eberhard Arnold*. New York: Paulist Press, 1984.

Johnson, Luke Timothy. *Living Jesus: Learning the Heart of the Gospel*. HarperSanFrancisco, 1998.

————. *The Real Jesus: The Misguided Quest for the Historical Jesus and the Truth of the Traditional Gospels*. Paperback edition. HarperSanFrancisco, 1997.

Käsemann, Ernst. *Commentary on Romans.* Trans. Geoffrey W. Bromiley. Grand Rapids: Wm. B. Eerdmans Publishing Co., 1980.

———. "The Eschatological Royal Reign of God." *Your Kingdom Come: Report on the World Conference on Mission and Evangelism,* pp. 61-71. Geneva: World Council of Churches, 1980.

Kenneson, Philip D., and James L. Street. *Selling Out the Church: The Dangers of Church Marketing.* Nashville: Abingdon Press, 1997.

Kierkegaard, Søren. *Eighteen Upbuilding Discourses for Self-Examination* and *Judge for Yourself.* Ed. and trans. Howard V. Hong and Edna H. Hong. Princeton: Princeton University Press, 1990.

———. *The Journals of Søren Kierkegaard.* Ed. and trans. Alexander Dru. London: Oxford University Press, 1938.

Langewiesche, William. "The Shipbreakers." *Atlantic Monthly* 286, no. 2 (August 2000): 31-49.

Lawrence, Roy. *Christian Healing Rediscovered.* Downers Grove, IL: InterVarsity Press, 1980.

Lenski, R. C. H. *The Interpretation of St. Paul's First and Second Epistles to the Corinthians.* Minneapolis: Augsburg Publishing House, 1937.

Lewis, C. S. "Evil and God." In *God in the Dock: Essays on Theology and Ethics,* ed. Walter Hooper, pp. 21-24. Grand Rapids: Wm. B. Eerdmans Publishing Co., 1970.

Lindbeck, George A. *The Nature of Doctrine: Religion and Theology in a Postliberal Age.* Philadelphia: Westminster Press, 1984.

Lischer, Richard. "Living by the Word: A Sense of Ending." *Christian Century* 116, no. 8 (10 March 1999): 277.

Louw, Johannes P., and Eugene A. Nida, eds. *Greek-English Lexicon of the New Testament Based on Semantic Domains.* Volumes 1 and 2. New York: United Bible Societies, 1988.

MacGregor, G. H. C. "Principalities and Powers: The Cosmic Background of Paul's Thought." *New Testament Studies* 1 (1954): 17-28.

Mackay, Hugh. *Turning Point: Australians Choosing Their Future.* Sydney: Pan Macmillan Australia, 1999.

Martin, Ralph P. *2 Corinthians.* Word Biblical Commentary. Waco, TX: Word Books, 1986.

Marty, Martin E. "'Who Is Jesus Christ for Us Today?' as Asked by Young People." In *Growing Up Postmodern: Imitating Christ in the Age of "Whatever,"* ed. Kenda Creasy Dean, pp. 21-28. Princeton, NJ: Institute for Youth Ministry, 1999.

Miller, Donald E. "The Reinvented Church: Styles and Strategies." *Christian Century* 116, no. 36 (22-29 Dec. 1999): 1250-53.

Moore, Charles E., ed. *Provocations: Spiritual Writings of Kierkegaard.* Farmington, PA: The Plough Publishing House, 1999.

Morgenthaler, Shirley K., ed. *Exploring Children's Spiritual Formation: Foundational Issues.* River Forest, IL: Pillars Press, 1999.

Morris, Leon. *The Cross in the New Testament.* 2nd ed. Grand Rapids: Wm. B. Eerdmans Publishing Co., 1999.

Morrison, Clinton D. *The Powers That Be: Earthly Rulers and Demonic Powers in Romans 13.1-7.* Studies in Biblical Theology No. 29. Naperville, IL: Alec R. Allenson, 1960.

Mouw, Richard J. *Politics and the Biblical Drama.* Grand Rapids: Wm. B. Eerdmans Publishing Co., 1976.

Murphy, Francis Xavier, C.SS.R. *Politics and the Early Christians.* New York: Desclee Company, 1967.

Olsen, Charles M. *Transforming Church Boards into Communities of Spiritual Leaders.* Bethesda, MD: Alban Institute, 1995.

Pohl, Christine D. *Making Room: Recovering Hospitality as a Christian Tradition.* Grand Rapids: Wm. B. Eerdmans Publishing Co., 1999.

Postman, Neil. *Amusing Ourselves to Death: Public Discourse in the Age of Show Business.* New York: Viking Penguin, 1985.

Rhoads, David, and Donald Michie. *Mark as Story: An Introduction to the Narrative of a Gospel.* Philadelphia: Fortress Press, 1982.

Rupp, Gordon. *Principalities and Powers: Studies in the Christian Conflict in History.* New York: Abingdon-Cokesbury Press, 1952.

Sarewitz, Daniel, and Roger Pielke Jr. "Breaking the Global-Warming Gridlock." *Atlantic Monthly* 286, no. 1 (July 2000): 54-64.

Savage, Timothy B. *Power Through Weakness: Paul's Understanding of the Christian Ministry in 2 Corinthians.* Society for New Testament Studies Monograph Series 86. Cambridge: Cambridge University Press, 1996.

Schlier, Heinrich. *Der Brief an die Epheser: Ein Kommentar.* 7th ed. Düsseldorf: Patmos, 1971.

———. *Principalities and Powers in the New Testament.* New York: Herder and Herder, 1961.

Schumacher, Frederick J., comp. and ed., with Dorothy A. Zelenko. *For All the Saints: A Prayer Book for and by the Church.* Volume 1: Year 1, Advent to the Day of Pentecost. Delhi, NY: American Lutheran Publicity Bureau, 1994.

Sider, Ron. *Just Generosity: A New Vision for Overcoming Poverty in America.* Grand Rapids: Baker Books, 1999.

Simpson, E. K., and F. F. Bruce. *Commentary on the Epistles to the Ephesians and the Colossians.* Grand Rapids: Wm. B. Eerdmans Publishing Co., 1957.

Stassen, Glen, ed. *Just Peacemaking: Ten Practices for Abolishing War.* Cleveland: Pilgrim Press, 1998.

Stewart, James S. "On a Neglected Emphasis in New Testament Theology." *Scottish Journal of Theology* 4, no. 3 (Sept. 1951): 292-301.

Stortz, Martha Ellen. *PastorPower*. Nashville: Abingdon Press, 1993.

Stott, John R. W. *God's New Society: The Message of Ephesians*. Downers Grove, IL: InterVarsity Press, 1979.

Stringfellow, William. *An Ethic for Christians and Other Aliens in a Strange Land.* Waco, TX: Word Books, 1973.

————. *Free in Obedience*. New York: Seabury Press, 1964.

Swartley, Willard M., ed. *Violence Renounced: René Girard, Biblical Studies, and Peacemaking*. Volume 4 of *Studies in Peace and Scripture*. Telford, PA: Pandora Press U.S., 2000.

Swoboda, Jörg. *The Revolution of the Candles: Christians in the Revolution of the German Democratic Republic*. Ed. Richard V. Pierard. Trans. Edwin P. Arnold. Macon, GA: Mercer University Press, 1996.

Taylor, Barbara Brown. "Preaching the Terrors." In *Exilic Preaching: Testimony for Christian Exiles in an Increasingly Hostile Culture,* ed. Erskine Clarke, pp. 83-90. Harrisburg, PA: Trinity Press International, 1998.

Trulear, Harold Dean. "Go and Do Likewise: The Church's Role in Caring for Crime Victims." In *God and the Victim: Theological Reflections on Evil, Victimization, Justice, and Forgiveness,* ed. Lisa Barnes Lampman and Michelle Shattuck, pp. 70-88. Grand Rapids: Wm. B. Eerdmans Publishing Co., 1999.

Van den Heuvel, Albert H. *These Rebellious Powers*. New York: Friendship Press, 1965.

Vanier, Jean. *The Heart of L'Arche: A Spirituality for Every Day*. New York: Crossroad, 1995.

Visser 't Hooft, W. A. *The Kingship of Christ: An Interpretation of Recent European Theology*. New York: Harper and Brothers, 1948.

Volf, Miroslav. "Faith Matters: Floating Along?" *Christian Century* 117, no. 11 (5 April 2000): 398.

Walsh, Brian, Richard Middleton, Mark Vander Vennen, and Sylvia Keesmaat. *The Advent of Justice: A Book of Meditations*. Sioux City, IA: Dordt College Press, 1993.

Wangerin, Walter, Jr. *Reliving the Passion: Meditations on the Suffering, Death, and Resurrection of Jesus as Recorded in Mark*. Grand Rapids: Zondervan Publishing House, 1992.

Webber, Robert E. *The Church in the World: Opposition, Tension, or Transformation*. Grand Rapids: Zondervan Academie Books, 1986.

Whiteley, D. E. H. *The Theology of St. Paul*. Oxford: Basil Blackwell, 1964.

Wilder, Amos N. *Kerygma, Eschatology, and Social Ethics*. Facet Books Social Ethics Series No. 12. Franklin Sherman, gen. ed. Philadelphia: Fortress Press, 1966.

Wink, Walter. *Engaging the Powers: Discernment and Resistance in a World of Domination.* Volume 3 of *The Powers.* Minneapolis: Fortress Press, 1992.

————. *Naming the Powers: The Language of Power in the New Testament.* Volume 1 of *The Powers.* Philadelphia: Fortress Press, 1984.

————. *The Powers That Be.* New York: Doubleday, 1999.

————. *Unmasking the Powers: The Invisible Forces that Determine Human Existence.* Volume 2 of *The Powers.* Philadelphia: Fortress Press, 1986.

————. *When the Powers Fall.* Minneapolis: Augsburg-Fortress, 1998.

Wolterstorff, Nicholas. "The Contours of Justice: An Ancient Call for Shalom." In *God and the Victim: Theological Reflections on Evil, Victimization, Justice, and Forgiveness,* ed. Lisa Barnes Lampman and Michelle Shattuck, pp. 116-37. Grand Rapids: Wm. B. Eerdmans Publishing Co., 1999.

Wylie Kellermann, Bill. "Not Vice Versa. Reading the Powers Biblically: Stringfellow, Hermeneutics, and the Principalities." *Anglican Theological Review* 81, no. 4 (1999): 665-82.

————. *Seasons of Faith and Conscience: Kairos, Confession, Liturgy.* Maryknoll, NY: Orbis Books, 1991.

Yates, Roy. "The Powers of Evil in the New Testament." *Evangelical Quarterly* 52 (1980): 97-111.

Yoder, John H. *He Came Preaching Peace.* Scottdale, PA: Herald Press, 1985.

————. *The Politics of Jesus.* 2nd ed. Grand Rapids: Wm. B. Eerdmans Publishing Company, 1994.

Yoder Neufeld, Thomas R. *Ephesians.* Believers Church Bible Commentary. Scottdale, PA: Herald Press, forthcoming.

————. *'Put on the Armour of God': The Divine Warrior from Isaiah to Ephesians.* Journal for the Study of the New Testament Supplement Series 140. Sheffield, England: Sheffield Academic Press, 1997.

Zehr, Howard. "Restoring Justice." In *God and the Victim: Theological Reflections on Evil, Victimization, Justice, and Forgiveness,* ed. Lisa Barnes Lampman and Michelle Shattuck, pp. 131-59. Grand Rapids: Wm. B. Eerdmans Publishing Co., 1999.

Zizioulas, John D. *Being as Communion: Studies in Personhood and the Church.* Crestwood, NY: St. Vladimir's Press, 1985.

Zuendel, Friedrich. *The Awakening: One Man's Battle with Darkness.* Farmington, PA: The Plough Publishing House, 1999.